No Place to Be
a Child

No Place to Be a Child

*Growing Up
in a War Zone*

by

James Garbarino
Kathleen Kostelny
Nancy Dubrow

Jossey-Bass Publishers • San Francisco

Jossey-Bass books and products are available through most bookstores. To contact Jossey-Bass directly, call (888) 378-2537, fax to (800) 605-2665, or visit our website at www.josseybass.com.

Substantial discounts on bulk quantities of Jossey-Bass books are available to corporations, professional associations, and other organizations. For details and discount information, contact the special sales department at Jossey-Bass.

For sales outside the United States, please contact your local Simon & Schuster International Office.

TCF Manufactured in the United States of America on Lyons Falls Turin Book. This paper is acid-free and 100 percent totally chlorine-free.

Library of Congress Cataloging-in-Publication Data

Garbarino, James.
   No place to be a child : growing up in a war zone / James
Garbarino, Kathleen Kostelny, Nancy Dubrow. — 1st ed.
     p.   cm.
   Originally published: Lexington, Mass. : Lexington Books, 1991.
   Includes bibliographical references (p.   ) and index.
   ISBN 0-7879-4375-4 (paperback : alk. paper)
   1. Children and war.   2. Children and violence.   I. Kostelny,
Kathleen.   II. Dubrow, Nancy.   III. Title.
HQ784.W3G37   1998
303.6'083—dc21   98-20012

HB Printing
10 9 8 7 6 5 4 3 2

PB Printing
10 9 8 7 6 5 4 3 2 1

This book is dedicated to the healers and the peacemakers,
the people who seek to make the world a better place
for children growing up in war zones.

Contents

Foreword by Liv Ullmann   ix
Preface and Acknowledgments   xix

1 Children and War   *1*

2 At What Cost?   *16*

3 Cambodian Survivors: Hell Is a Time and Place   *31*

4 Mozambique's Children: Dying Is the Easy Part   *60*

5 Nicaragua in Conflict: The Politics of Suffering   *83*

6 Palestinians in Revolt: Children of the *Intifada*   *101*

7 Chicago: The War Close to Home   *130*

8 Making a Place for Children Who Have No Place
       to Be a Child   *150*

Postscript   165
References   167
Index   173
About the Authors   179

Foreword

LIV ULLMANN

One-third of the world's nations engage in torture as a standard of the government. Most of the world engages one way or another in war or preparation for war. We live in a century where the leaders describe the strength of their country by announcing the number of missiles directed at another country.

At the same time there are more important words and statements that seldom make the headlines. These are voices of children. In an overcrowded refugee camp in Thailand, a little boy confides to the visitor: "Sometimes I want to cry. But I don't want other children to see it. So I cry only when it rains."

Every day nearly 40,000 children die from deprivation. That means one child every other second. That means now—and now—and now—and. . . .

What can we as individuals do? We can finally rise and say "Enough." For millions of children it is already too late, but there is still time to save millions more.

It is for all of us—we who have inherited the awful legacy of the Holocaust—to decide by our action that this shall happen "never again." It is for all of us to share the knowledge with each other that we have *learned* the lesson of the Holocaust: that wherever and whenever any man or woman's freedom is diminished, any child's life is threatened, *there,* we know, that *our* freedom is diminished, *our* rights are denied, *our* life is threatened. And we will not wait until we hear the knock upon our own door!

An image from the Second World War: "Then the guard ordered the children to fold their clothes neatly and march into the gas chamber and crematorium. One little boy, less than two years old, was too little to climb the steps. The guard took the child in his arms and carried him into the gas chamber." This little boy died in vain if we sit back and let it happen over and over again, only in different ways. In Cambodia, Nicaragua, Mozambique, and the Middle East, the story is repeated. *All* war is war against children!

We have to give an answer to history's assault upon the dignity of little girls and boys. Despite all that is done to cheapen their lives, we must insist that each life is unique. That life is sacred. That each individual has within him or her the capacity of making a vital difference in the world.

We have to remind ourselves and the rest of the world that those who are indifferent to children's misery are as responsible as those who inflict it. As Elie Wiesel, himself a "child of war," has said: "More than anything—more than hatred and torture—more than pain—do I fear the world's indifference."

I don't believe we will love our own country and our own children less—only perhaps in a different way—if at the same time that we love our own, we also learn to understand the love of others for *their* country and *their* children.

No more to be satisfied by giving money or a moment's sympathy to a tragedy that is distant—but to feel from within that I am part of the whole world. Not only *feel* this—but really *know* it.

I will never forget the doctors and nurses I have met in the poorest of countries, who left brilliant, well-paid careers, to work seven days a week in refugee camps, some of them without pay at all, just because they decided to do what their conscience and their heart and their humanity told them to do. Nor will I forget the priests and nuns I met in the most deprived communities, who didn't *preach* love—who *acted* love.

And I won't forget the young people I have met in the refugee camps in all corners of the world, the *volunteers*. Some of them had been drifters, on drugs—like the twenty-year-old boy who one day saw a picture of a little baby, all skin and bones, and decided to go to see if he could be of any help. He's still there in a refugee camp in Thailand, but today he's off drugs, and his life has a meaning. Or a girl I hear about, fifteen years old, who came to the same camp with her mother and father who are doctors. She was told she was too young to do anything. But she wasn't. She carried all the old people too weak to move themselves to the toilets, and helped them, and washed them, and carried them back. We will all be better because of that fifteen-year-old girl.

And I won't forget a woman, who, in her mind, had left our world and gone into another. No one knew what she'd been through. She was crying, and the only thing that would stop her crying was someone holding her. The moment one let go, she started to cry again. But there were always arms to hold her, kind hands to wipe her tears. Not all were that lucky.

A bed, smaller than the one I have in my apartment, is the *home* of a family of seven—not only the *people,* but all their *belongings* as well. *One* bed for *seven* people. And if a family consists of only *two,* they will have to share the bed, the home, with another family.

The knowledge how much even a touch means when you are in need.

I remember a paper I saw plastered on a wall of one of the camps: "Sympathy is not enough, but it is a good beginning." There are many ways to begin. One of them is to believe that the world needn't be evil simply because some people are. It is only evil when we let the evil happen. When the good man allows evil.

It is my belief that I will never have fulfilled my potential so long as I have something of value to contribute to others. But my compassion, unlike my pity, must have a connection to the way I live, the way I make my plans, the way I make my choices.

While I am writing now, little boys and girls are dying as unknown to us in death as they were in life. But to those who loved them and gave them life, they are not faceless, they are not mere statistics. They are "son" and "daughter."

Does it make us say, "Such is the human race"? Or does it make us understand that we are not only *witnesses,* we are also participants?

Our grandparents were lucky. A hundred years ago, to hear news of disaster in faraway countries, they had to wait for the arrival of a traveler who took months to report to a shocked world what he had seen. Yes, they were lucky. For news reached them too late for anything to be done. Their consciences were clear.

Ours are not.

Are we going to say, as we said after the Second World War— after the destiny of six million Jewish people became part of our conscience and millions of Poles and Gypsies and—oh, I could go on and on. Are we going to say that we did not know; we did not see; we did not hear? What will our grandchildren, our great-grandchildren say about us, fifty years from now? Our action or lack of action today will describe *who* we were.

The Danish author V. K. Sorensen writes about *his* memory from the Second World War: "They shot my boy. He had done nothing. They came and shouted: 'Away with all the women and children.' The *men* were placed with their backs to the walls. But my boy—he was a child. He was fourteen years old. They hit him. They hit my son. I begged them not to shoot him. They shot him from behind. He ended his life at fourteen" (Sorensen 1945, 37).

We are all free men and free women. Or are we?

What about those who have no freedom? What about those who live as prisoners because of their beliefs or their race. What about those who have no freedom of choice because they are forced to live in hunger or without education? What about all the children in refugee camps and the homeless children of the streets?

Will they see us and know that we have not forgotten? Will they know that we have not abandoned them? Will they know that our pledge was true when we said, "Never again"?

Enough.

Most of the world *is* aware of poverty and hunger and disease. Most of the world is aware that people—and especially children—are dying or growing up weak and stunted and maimed. In the last ten years some 150 million children around the world have not grown up. They have died *wrenching, agonizing deaths.* And at least another 150 million have been disabled. *Crippled, maimed, stunted, dulled.* In terms of numbers this is *as if* every American and Canadian—250 million—born in the last ten years were now either dead or crippled!

We all share humanity's vulnerability to disaster and deprivation. In Bhopal, India, when the poisonous gases were carried by the wind, which way the wind was blowing was all that determined who was to die and who was to live. No one really knows where the earthquake, the flood, or the missile will strike the next time.

"Any man's death diminishes me," John Donne said. Yes, any man's death makes me smaller, less than I was before I learned of the death. *Any suffering or neglect I choose to turn away from defines me as a human being.*

I visited a refugee camp in Thailand the day after it had been shelled, shelling of unarmed victims. Eight people died and many more were wounded. In the primitive hospital were lying two little boys. They had lost their mother the night before. One was not expected to survive because his kidney and his liver were destroyed. The other little one had his tummy exchanged for a plastic bag on the outside of his body.

I think of the face of the little African boy from Sierra Leone who slept on the dirty pavement outside a cinema. Big posters on the walls above his head urged people to see *Rambo*. Torn, used tickets blowing in the sudden wind over the tired body of a child.

Think of the face you love the most, your own child. . . .

Perhaps we are simply fortunate to be chosen as those actors who have the opportunity to play out this chapter in history—when there are such tragedies but also such possibilities to improve life. Our choice now is whether or not to accept our role. I urge you to join the cast of those who listen, who care, who act.

I remember a little boy without a mother who walked away with an empty plate. His behind was as wrinkled as an old man's.

I remember a mother who watched her child die in her arms.

I know another mother. Me. She has one child. I used to hope and pray that others would always show my child compassion. Today my hope is different: I believe the most important thing I can wish for her is that *she* will meet *other people* with compassion.

There are two lives to each of us: the life of our actions and the life of our minds and hearts. We can allow these lives to exist together. Because we live in deeds and not in years; because we live in thoughts and feelings, not in figures and possessions. Time is counted by our heartbeats. And he or she lives the most who feels the noblest and acts the best.

I think of my grandmother. The silvery hair of many years, shining around a face marked lovingly by life. And that half-smile, mysterious and wise. My grandmother, my best friend, my storyteller, my teacher. She re-created the world, making it a wonderful place in which everything might happen. In which a tree or a stone was so much more than what we could see with our eyes. I would paint for her—I would paint a tree that was a black dot with a lot of red things around it, and she would smile and say: "How lovely! What a beautiful tree!" And only when the other grown-ups told me that trees did not look like that did I look at my dots and decide that painting wasn't for me.

With my grandmother, I explored all I did not know. She showed me how the veins in the leaves were alive and pulsating, and she was the first to tell me that plants cried out when you hurt them. Everything that grew had its beauty, a life of its own. We never spoke of conservation, but Grandmother taught me that I had no right to dominate nature, violate it, as if I were not responsible for the whole.

She would sing for me. And sitting on her lap—in the nape of her neck, I would find the sweet and dusty smell that I shall never forget—and which I only found again many years later on someone else.

It was the *wholeness* of life she wished for me, because life, to her, was never divided into compartments with different labels. To her, there was a coherent meaning given to all aspects of living. Or, to paraphrase Robert Frost, a life where "Love and need are one."

One day she was no more. And nothing was ever the same.

I traveled the world and became a well-known actress, but deep down I was always mourning that she was not there to share my life with me. To comment on it. Then, ten years ago, I traveled to the island of Macao. Refugees from Vietnam had arrived there in overloaded vessels. Terrified and often speechless survivors. In the middle of the refugee camp was a shelter for lepers, tended by nuns in long gray dresses that rustled in the heat. Inside I stopped in front of an old woman lying in a fetal position on her mattress. Her thin, sorrowful moans were the only sound in the room. For a long time I just stood staring at her, helpless, disgusted even, my arms hanging at my sides. Not daring to *touch*. A passing nun gave me a little pat on the shoulder and nodded toward the woman who had no fingers and no toes and half of her face eaten away.

I slowly bent down.

My arms enveloped the woman.

The smell in the nape of her neck.

My grandmother's.

Gently I stroked her.

Grey silver hair in a long braid. Slender shoulders.

My grandmother—I remembered there and then—how *her* arms felt around me—the scent of her skin.

The moment I touched the old woman from Vietnam, she gave a little sigh of relief. Something changed for me that day: I became a *grown-up*—understanding suddenly that *learning* is to *listen*.

More than ever do we need to define strength, not as descriptive of how far and how fast a man can run, or how far a country can send a missile, or how strong its destructiveness will be, but in what ways we, as people, show strength by our vision, and by *acting* upon it. A vision that encompasses other people sharing our time on earth.

The right to be recognized as a human being is the first right. And everyone must not only *know* this truth but live by it, because everyone is as real to himself as I am to myself.

I question and even dismiss the common values of today that represent old patriarchal thinking based on dominance and conquest. Values that belong to a mechanical and technological world where everything can be taken to pieces and put back together again with new pieces, instead of a world where *all* is considered part of, and unique for, the *whole*.

I trust that a world where priorities are given to nurturing, holding, and embracing would be a better world for all. A world where such values, when called for, even by a man, are not considered "naive." A world celebrating so-called traditional female values.

This means that we, women, as individuals, must learn how to *emphasize* our uniqueness, *cherish* our uniqueness, and learn never to *undervalue* ourselves. And offer men the joy of sharing this strength and knowledge with us.

I trust in our power to trace the time when we were of a pure heart, when as children we painted strange trees and spoke with the flowers. When we *touched* without fear.

I believe that the details of our lives will be forgotten by most, but the *emotion*, the *spirit*, will linger with those who shared it, and be part of them forever.

My daughter taught me an important lesson: "Let us dare to use our *own* language—which in politics especially, would be a new kind of language, descriptive of real feelings. So as no longer to be dismissed, for example, as 'the starving Africans' or 'economic refugees,' we need to explore with each other and our children the richness and color and history and art which prevail in other countries. Be more sensitive in our use of language—and thus more sensitive human beings."

Not long ago, with a small group of women, I visited some "detention centers" for Vietnamese refugees in Hong Kong. Our time there was deliberately limited. Most press people, most civilians were denied entry into these "jails." The only journalists who seemed welcome to the camps were writers who described a refugee like this—and I quote from newspapers in Hong Kong at the time of our visit—as "thuggish individuals" or "human vermin."

Men, women, and children who were given numbers and not allowed to keep their names once they entered the camps. Thus so much easier to think of and treat them as *less* than human. It has been tried before with "success" by Hitler's Nazi soldiers. Today we are succeeding even more easily—to write the history of refugees as if *their* history is not ours, their future of less concern—because they are simply numbers, statistics. Their life and misery "self-inflicted" as if *we* were witnesses only.

So easily we forget—that those who survive will carry the mark for life. And so will we.

Let us dare to make *solutions* based on *compassion,* even if such an initiative may sound naive.

Native American men and women never made an important decision without thinking about the consequences of this decision for the seventh generation of their descendants. *Today* decisions or program evaluations or promises are too often made so that they will look good until the next board meeting or the next election.

Slogans instead of visions.

Media attention focused on statesmen attending summits instead of children struggling for their lives.

I trust us to finally say "Enough." Change the language. Because there are more important priorities. There are opportunities waiting for us all. Voices we must listen to. People, real human beings out there in the world who will *not* vote for us today or applaud us today or honor us today: The little ones. The weak. The deprived. The message—on their behalf—that we must deliver again and again. The priority we must give the needs of children.

We will finally be described—defined—by how we reacted to their needs. The finished portrait of ourselves that we cannot change, however beautifully ornamented the frame. The finished portrait of ourselves will encompass the care and the vision enacted by us on behalf of *them*.

Today we know how to reach the stars, how to land on the moon and encircle the earth. But we know so little about how to reach each other. Touch each other.

Through the destinies of others, that will be known to us—destinies we cannot turn off by changing the channel on our TV or wipe away as a tear and go on with our lives—through the destinies of other women and children and men and families, we will recognize ourselves and learn that we are not *witnesses* only to their fates.

We are participants.

More and more we will learn to *trust* that to give way to one's feelings is a great ease to one's heart. The strongest woman *or* man is the one who knows how to love.

The people all around you now—take a good look at them. Because when you later make a choice in life, *they* are included as well; whether your choice is one of indifference or one of love.

There are no choices made by individuals that do not include others.

So many stories I could have told—I'm surrounded by invisible—to us right now—little children. Surrounded by women who need us if they are to go on with their lives. They are not numbers. They are not faceless. In fact, they are you and me, and eventually we will *all* be counted together.

Because we live in deeds and not in years. We live in our thoughts, we live in our feelings—not in figures and possessions. Time is counted by our heartbeats. And he or she lives the most who *feels* the noblest and *acts* the best.

In their book *No Place to Be a Child*, Jim, Kathleen, and Nancy have made a journey, a journey of discoveries to understand the experience of growing up in a war zone. It is a journey to discover what it means to be a citizen in a world of people who too often close their eyes and ears to the voices of children and parents caught in the cross fire. It is a journey each of us may make one way or another if we are to become authentic human beings. To become authentic while listening to the children who share our time on earth—and really hear them.

Please listen to a child, living behind barbed wire in one of the "concentration camps" in Hong Kong. A sixteen-year-old refugee from Vietnam, he speaks for the children of war when he writes the the following poem:

I Am Sorrow

Who will listen to my feeling?
Who will listen to my useless land?
After the war, my skin had been damaged,
There are craters in my body.
Although I was sad, sorry, and suffering
Who will listen to my feeling?
I am sad, sorry, and suffering
Who will know my feeling?
I am not sad about my harmed body
I am sorrow because of the people
   who can't use me rightly.
Who will know my feeling?

Sindy Cheung, 3 May 1989

Preface and Acknowledgments

Without even knowing it, we were preparing ourselves to write this book for more than two decades. As the offspring of parents who came to adulthood during World War II, we grew from adolescence to adulthood during the Vietnam War. The contrast between those two wars—one the "Good War" and the other the "Bad War"—stimulated debates in our country and in our families. These debates did much to shape our thoughts and feelings about war, and to lay the groundwork for what we have written here.

Since becoming adults, we have committed our professional lives to children, as teachers, therapists, researchers, and advocates working in more than a dozen institutions, from universities and research centers to settlement houses and therapeutic schools.

Our experiences working together at Erikson Institute for Advanced Study in Child Development in Chicago led us to explore the situation of children growing up in danger because of chronic community violence. Our firsthand experience with children growing up in inner-city America was the starting point for thinking about what it means for children to live in a war zone.

Our first trip to the Middle East in January 1988, to observe the role of children in the Israeli-Palestinian conflict, was the catalyst for writing this book. Our experience in the Middle East prompted us to begin thinking about the similarities and differences of children living in war zones defined by political conflict and children living in American urban war zones defined by crime, drugs, and poverty.

With our professional expertise and personal experiences as a foundation, we set out on a series of journeys. We selected five war zones around the world. These included inner-city Chicago, where violence associated with gang warfare had reached unprecedented levels. Our first visit to the Middle East led to a second and a more systematic look at the Palestinian rebellion in the Occupied Territories known as the *Intifada*. We added to these experiences visits to Africa, Asia, and Central America. In Africa we chose Mozambique as the site for our investigations. Mozambique had suffered through more than a decade of sustained military conflict, including wanton and bestial attacks on civilians by the antigovernment Renamo terrorist organization. In Asia, we traveled to Cambodia. Few countries have experienced such a national trauma as occurred in Cambodia before, during, and after the genocidal regime of Pol Pot's Khmer Rouge from 1975 to 1979. When we visited Cambodia in 1990, the civil war that had been dormant for a few years was heating up again. In Central America, we selected Nicaragua. We visited Nicaragua just as a decade of military conflict between the Sandinista government and the Contras was coming to an end in the wake of national elections in 1990 and was giving way to intense nonmilitary political conflict.

We went to these war zones as child development professionals seeking to understand their children from a clinical perspective. In all five places we prepared ourselves by reviewing existing research and clinical reports on the experience of children and parents. During our visits we interviewed children, youth, parents, teachers, social workers, physicians, nurses, psychologists, community leaders, soldiers, and others who could shed light on the experience of children growing up in a war zone. We asked children to draw pictures of their homes and their communities, asked them to tell us what these pictures meant to them, and asked what it was like to live in their homes and their communities.

We learned that most children can cope with horrible experiences and high levels of stress if they have a secure relationship with parents or effective substitutes, and if these adults themselves can continue to function as sources of support and encouragement for "their" children. We learned that resilient children do cope, but not without cost. Even when they survive reasonably intact, they may face lifelong challenges as a result of growing up in a war zone. These challenges include threats to their mental health, to their physical well-being, and to their moral development.

We returned home with these clinical conclusions. But as we made our journey we moved beyond our clinical interests to a broader arena. We came to see ever more clearly the insidiousness of political labels that often hide and obscure the real meaning of war for kids.

We saw clearly the folly and maliciousness of allowing governments—including our own—to hide behind these labels. When we look at the children of war, we do not see "Communist children" or "capitalist children" or "Sandinista children" or "Contra children" or "PLO children" or "Zionist children" or "progovernment children" or "subversive children." We only see children.

This recognition became all the more important to us when Iraqi military forces invaded and occupied Kuwait just as we were finishing this book in 1990. We watched the world grope for a moral response, and we were fearful of the consequences. We shuddered as our country rang with calls to "bomb Baghdad," as if this somehow meant something different from killing, maiming, and orphaning more children. January 16, 1991 realized our worst fears.

If we learned anything from our journey, it is that each of us has the responsibility to see things clearly. As citizens of our own beloved United States, we are responsible for the havoc wrought in our names through the application of military force in Central America, in Southeast Asia, and in every other region of the world where we are supplying the armaments to sustain war, even when we are not the ones pulling the triggers. As citizens of the world, we learned to value above all else the healers and the peacemakers who try to make the hurt go away for the children of war, and we aspired to join their ranks. This book is part of that commitment. Writing it helped us to feel whole.

But this was a costly book to write. It cost time and money and pain and fear.

Time. Behind the many hours spent writing were the days spent traveling and the months spent visiting war zones, on airplanes, and in taxis, buses, trucks, boats, trains, motorbikes, pedicabs, and on foot. Time spent away from home, family, and friends, often in uncomfortable circumstances. Time spent waiting to make arrangements. Time spent getting there. Time spent getting around. Time spent recuperating.

Money. Travel to places like Mozambique, Cambodia, Nicaragua, and the Middle East is expensive. And it costs money to prepare for such travel, to live in a foreign country, and to spend time at home digesting what you have learned in your travels. Our special thanks go to the people and foundations that sponsored our work. They know who they are. Of course, we, not they, are responsible for the conclusions we have drawn, the observations we have made, and the indignation we have expressed in our criticisms of American policy and practice regarding war.

Pain. We have seen and heard (and experienced) much personal pain in the writing of this book. Adults and children shared their pain with us. For that sharing we are grateful, and we hope we have done justice to our informants. Indeed, "doing justice" to the children of war zones became our passion as we wrote this book. Our moral obligation made it clear to us that the story we wanted to tell would not be simply "clinical" in the sense of describing and analyzing the psychological development of children in war zones. Keeping faith with the children meant trying to make sense of their experience in the life of our nation. This belief led us to make some stiff criticisms of our country's policies. It made this a very "political" book in ways that make some people uncomfortable.

Fear. It was frightening to ally ourselves with the children of war. It sometimes meant putting ourselves in harm's way. We did so as cautiously as we could, in respect for our responsibilities to our own families, our own loved ones, spouses, "significant others," and offspring. Our mothers and fathers agonized every minute we were away, as would any parent whose child comes in contact with war. And each of them breathed a deep sigh of relief when the final trip was over.

At various times while researching and writing this book we were under surveillance by at least one country's intelligence service, were detained or questioned by soldiers and police, were in places that were officially "off limits" to us and thereby risked legal consequences or worse, were intimidated by gangs of one sort or another, or were in the vicinity of shooting. Of course, many people have been in much greater danger, and many people live with such danger on a daily basis. But even our relatively tame brushes with physical danger were frightening.

Our thanks go to the healers and the peacemakers who facilitated our visits and who shared their stories and their expertise with us. Some of these people must remain unnamed here to protect their security. Some we can mention here, and apologize in advance to those whose names we inadvertently omitted.

Cambodia: Cheryle Lipsky, John McAuliff, Laura McGrew, Kao Samreth, Beat Schweitzer, Joan Seeler, Lorna Stevens, and Susan Walker.

Chicago: Carl Bell, Jane Grady, Alex Kotlowitz, Carole Pardo and the Lutheran Social Services of Illinois, Frank Seever and the Chicago Commons Association.

Mozambique: Neil Boothby, Ambassador Ferrao, Francisca Mawriccio, the Mozambique Support Network, Prexy Nesbitt, Mark van Hoovering and the Christian Council of Mozambique, Bridget Walker, and Mary Yarwood.

Nicaragua: Ann Coyne, Rosario Diaz, Jose and Olga Frech, Carlos Palacios, Marcia Ramirez, Marilyn Rocky, and Susana Vogel.

Palestine: Cairo Arafat, Jennifer Bing-Canar, Mark Brown, Assia Habash and the staff of the Early Childhood Resource Center, Anne Nixon, and John Woods.

Special thanks go to UNICEF staff at United Nations Headquarters in New York and the international field offices.

And our thanks go to those supporters and colleagues at Erikson Institute and at other institutions around the country who helped us with the intellectual content and the work of manuscript preparation. Among these helpful individuals were Jane Curry, Robert Halpern, Ned Hanauer, Irving Harris, Jane Power, Norma Richman, Dan Scheinfeld, Ellen Siegel, Fran Stott, Carla Young, and Margaret Zusky. We hasten to make clear that we, not they, are responsible for this book, knowing that some readers will find some of our observations and conclusions "controversial." So be it.

No Place to Be
a Child

Children and War

As you read this, tens of thousands of children are facing danger in war zones around the world. These war zones are not associated with the kinds of big wars that dominate the history books we read in school. Mostly small wars dominate today's landscape: civil wars, insurrections, border disputes, the stuff that makes the front pages for a day or two once a year when something extraordinary happens, then gets buried in the back pages or is totally ignored until the conflict produces something else that is "newsworthy" for the American public. Other children are facing danger in America's "war zones," with their poverty, crime, and drugs.

According to UNICEF estimates (UNICEF 1986), about 80 percent of the casualties in these foreign wars are women and children. Women and children suffer disproportionately when warring groups seek to control "the hearts and minds" of a populace. That children survive at all in the heat of war is testimony to their resilience and to the efforts of the adults who care for them: parents, teachers, relatives, friends, and therapists.

We set out on a journey of discovery that took us to five war zones around the world. Each has its own special character, its own local issues. But each forced us to confront children and adults coping with terror and dislocation and loss. As child development professionals we set out to understand the experience of growing up in war zones. We brought to this challenge our understanding of the social, emotional, and intellectual development of children and our knowledge of the roles parents and other adults play in promoting and preserving that development. And we also brought our identities as

Americans whose youth was shaped by the Vietnam War, Americans born to parents who lived through World War II.

We set out to make sense of the experience of children in war as best we could with what we knew and what we believed about children and families, and about war. We started our journey as innocents concerning what war means for those who live through it. We ended that journey changed forever by our experiences. Even our partial glimpses into the experience of growing up in a war zone left us pained, shaken, and angry, angry because there is so much suffering in the world and because so much of that suffering continues as a matter of conscious policy, policy for which we as citizens of the world are responsible.

Getting to know the children of war has pushed us to the very limits of human experience. It has challenged *and* affirmed our conception of what it means to be a child, indeed, of what it means to be a human being. Like any journey of importance, it has taught us as much about ourselves as about anyone or anything else.

Our own childhoods had their triumphs and disappointments. We experienced threats and opportunities. We got sick and recovered. We were frightened and were comforted. Our nation was at war: cold war, hot war, cold war again. We grew up with the specter of atomic war, and we practiced "duck and cover" drills at school in anticipation of a bright flash in the sky that would mean "it" had finally happened. We played at war—mainly a child-sized replica of World War II, complete with "Nazis" and "Japs." We grew through adolescence and into adulthood in a nation dominated by the images and realities of the Vietnam War in which some friends and acquaintances fought and died and others protested (and went to jail or left the country).

Yes, we knew of war. But real war took place far away from our homes. We had images of war, but we had real childhoods. We had childhoods that were profoundly normal and safe in contrast to those of the children we have come to know in war zones around the world and in some inner-city neighborhoods of our own country. As we think of these children, we find ourselves returning again and again to the eerie words written by Stephanie Urdang in her book about Mozambique, *And Still They Dance*. She wrote of a war-ravaged child, "He had experienced more than one could ever dread for a child of that age." *More than one could ever dread.*

Every parent knows about dread. You read about the one in a million chance that your child will have a fatal reaction to a routine injection. You hear the screech of brakes and car tires while your child is playing out front, near the street. You calculate the odds of birth defects over and over again during nine months of pregnancy. You learn from your pediatrician that your child has what may be the early signs of leukemia. Drugs. Suicide. Abduction. Molestation. Drowning. Fire. Disfigurement. Yes, American parents know about dread. But most of us can take a deep, rational breath and relax in the knowledge that the odds against these dreaded outcomes are very much on our side.

A recent national survey of parents found that when asked to list the things they worried about most concerning their children, kidnapping topped the list. These parents should be rationally reassured to know that of all the tens of millions of children in the United States, the number kidnapped by a stranger in a given year is about one hundred.

Of all possible dangers, few ever touch most of us. But not in a war zone. In a war zone, particularly in today's war zones, the realities are sometimes worse than your worst imaginings. What American parent has to worry about a child stepping on a land mine and becoming legless, or being hit by a grenade on the way to school and killed? These things have happened in war zones; they still happen; they will happen again as you read this page. In a war zone, reality transcends the darkest imagination.

We came to dread much for the children we met as we traveled about the world. As we compared notes on our experiences, each of us could point to some worst case, when we felt ashamed that we humans could do such things to our fellow humans, and most particularly to our children.

Jim: "I think often about that little boy in the hospital in Mozambique who had been blinded and crippled by the explosion of a mine. He lay there alone, and curled up in a fetal position. His future? I can't bear to think, but I can recall the image with only the smallest effort—and sometimes it comes even without trying."

Kathleen: "I frequently remember Mansur operating his wheelchair with one arm, his other arm and both his legs blown off, completely blinded in one eye, and partially blinded in the other. I remember going into his hospital room in Jerusalem with presents—books, markers, marbles. But they were useless for a child who couldn't see, write, or even play the normal games of childhood. His childhood had been stolen from him in the seconds that it takes a grenade to explode."

Nancy: "In Chicago we met a two-year-old boy whose uncle was literally shot out from underneath him by a bullet. As the uncle carried the child on a walk through a public housing development, shots rang out, the uncle collapsed on the ground, and the child fell to the ground. How secure does this child of the urban war zone feel? Does anyone comprehend the war close to home?"

These children had indeed experienced "more than one could ever dread."

But we also found children of triumph, children who have struggled with the terror and the deprivation of war and have emerged with beauty of spirit. War is hell, but even in hell it seems that some children manage to construct some small place to be a child.

Kathleen: "In Nicaragua we met a girl whose parents had been kidnapped and killed. Now she was living with her adoptive family. She was doing well in school and wants to be a pediatrician when she grows up. She is active in a local youth organization. She still feels deeply the loss of her parents, but does not want revenge. She says there has been too much killing already and that it should just stop."

Nancy: "In the aftermath of war, children in Cambodia create inventions, dramatic play props, and games with materials they find in the streets. This is true for the children who are well and safe. Evident in their creativity is the capacity for development, given the opportunity. This gives us hope in spite of all the other children who are too sick to play and too terrified to relate to other children and adults. So many have sacrificed even the small pleasures of childhood."

Jim: "In the hospital in Mozambique there was a boy with a shattered leg—it was ugly to look at. But this boy was smiling. He had been through a lot of pain, and there was more to come, but he was smiling. His leg was mangled, but his life was intact. It reminded me of what really matters in making a human life livable. He made real everything I had ever read about 'coping' and 'resilience.' His family was around, and he seemed a spunky kid who had plenty of personal resources. He was an obvious favorite of the staff. I was grateful to him. Remembering him helped me deal with all the haunting, the haunting of the children who weren't going to make it, whose lives were a shambles."

A Matter of Time

There are 525,600 minutes in a year. How many of them are likely to have a lasting impact on a child? Cumulatively, many will, of course. For a child, the thousands of minutes spent basking in the glow of being loved tenderly add up. The total number of minutes spent reading or being read to matters; thousands of minutes are much better than hundreds. The minutes spent watching television—about 50,000 for many American children—exert an effect (and not generally a very positive effect, if truth be told).

How many minutes of war does it take to have an effect on a child? More than most experiences, the experience of war packs a great deal of power into a small amount of time. Only a few moments of war experience can produce images of such power that they reverberate over weeks, months, years . . . over a lifetime perhaps.

We understand that war means different things to different people. If we are honest, we must recognize that war may mean the fun and the adventure of being young and set loose on the world. This is one of war's attractions for young people, particularly young people who are trapped in a dead-end existence or who yearn for glory and excitement. For others, war may actually mean a more comfortable life. For example, people working in a munitions factory may earn higher wages than ever before because the factory supplies distant armies. We say this truth without trying to belittle or degrade people employed by the "defense industry." It is a fact that wars and misery in foreign countries can produce prosperity for many Americans.

Those who have been touched by direct encounters with war have vivid images of those encounters that stick with them, though they occupied but brief moments in a long life. Real war is like that. Soldiers who have seen combat report that war is mostly waiting for something to happen, and once it happens praying for the horror to stop. And then waiting for the power of its impact on the psyche to fade, or at least recede enough for life to go forward.

A soldier friend of ours recalls sending his comrade in arms across a bridge with fond, warm words and then only moments later recognizing his friend's body coming back under a plastic cover on a jeep. He recognized him by his boots. The image will last forever.

How many minutes does it take to create a permanent confrontation between children and their memories? Not many. Of the 525,600 minutes in a year, a handful will suffice. Those few can create a social and psychological reality that will dominate all others.

We met a boy in a hospital in Africa who one minute was leading a productive life as a herder of cows and who the next minute was a blind beggar because he stepped on a land mine planted by antigovernment bandits. It takes only a handful of minutes in war to change the course of a lifetime. It takes only an instant to become a cripple.

This is even more true of today's brand of wars than it was of the past's "conventional" wars. Today's wars are likely to put children in the front lines because there are no real front lines, only shifting zones of conflict. Days or even weeks may pass with objective peace, and yet past and future attacks set the tone for experiencing day-to-day life. We have seen and felt this reality during our own visits to war zones.

Spending a night in a Palestinian refugee camp under curfew is a visit to a war zone even if one does not experience rock throwing or Molotov cocktail tossing or shooting or midnight visits from soldiers on that particular night. What matters is knowing that any of these things could happen, not as some remote possibility like the possibility that armed bandits could break into your house in a middle-class suburb, but as something that happens frequently and will happen again.

Walking clandestinely from one house to another your host tells you, "Be very quiet. They can shoot at anyone out like this after curfew." The situation sounds melodramatic to be sure. But war zones convert the stuff of melodrama into reality.

In Nicaragua we rode in the back of a Sandinista government pickup truck through the night from a provincial town to the capital, Managua. We knew there had been Contra attacks on the road in the past, and that government vehicles were common Contra targets. But we reassured ourselves: "Why, of all nights, should this particular night be one of the nights for an attack?" The odds were comforting. We weren't really taking a chance. Weeks could pass between attacks. But even for us, we who had never been attacked, the fear was real enough. We weren't attacked; the only real danger we encountered that night was the traffic on the highway.

The next night a government vehicle was attacked on that same highway and people were killed.

What if we were Nicaraguan children who had encountered a few minutes out of the 525,600 that year when the bullets came? What good are the odds for such children? What good are the days and maybe even weeks when there are no real bullets in the air but bullets continue to exist in the imagination fed by memory?

War involves marching, and organizing, and waiting, and camaraderie, and movement, and laughing, and training, and adventure, and waste, and nobility. But what war is really about is destroying people. Tacticians tell us that it is preferable to wound than to kill, because the wounded require care and thus occupy resources, while the dead do not require much of anything. What is more, the wounded draw down the morale of the survivors.

War is about attacking the sack of fluids and solids in which we human beings transport our minds and souls. In his novel *Catch 22* Joseph Heller called this "Snowden's Secret." When the hot metal of bullets and bombs confronts the human body, life is revealed as a precious glimmer suspended in a lumpy soup supported by fragile bones.

War Is Not Like Anything

For most of us, the experience of war is remote and cushioned by comforting euphemisms. Our conception of war is sanitized by images associated with words like glory, struggle, patriotism, bravery, casualties, national security, collateral damage, victory, and defeat. As those who have been there tell us, however, the real essence of real war is terror, dismemberment, disfigurement, peeing in your pants from fear, being splattered with the guts of your friends, chaos so profound you can hardly bear to recognize it for what it is. When asked, "What was it like?" one soldier replied bitterly, "It's not *like* anything. It just is."

Or think of what "the body count" means to a child whose mother is one of those statistics. In their efforts to subdue the rebels in Afghanistan, an effort comparable in many ways to the efforts of the United States in Vietnam, Soviet forces lost 15,000 of their own troops dead; through their bombing, the Soviets obliterated more than half of Afghanistan's 30,000 villages. All in all, about 1.3 million were killed—most of them women and children. Why? It was a matter of strategic interest.

Strategy and games and power politics. All these stand in the way of really seeing. When you really see, you truly mourn the loss. As one Soviet official said as he toured the destruction wrought in his name by his government, "Look what we have done. My God, how are we ever to be forgiven?" (quoted in Burns 1990).

Each number in the real body count represents a hole in the life of some children—a mother, father, brother, sister, aunt, uncle, or cousin ripped away. Vietnam. Cambodia. Iran. Iraq. El Salvador. Germany. Korea. Poland. Romania. Kuwait. Is there any end to the list? You can choose by closing your eyes and stabbing your finger at any map. It seems that no country is immune to this game adults play with the lives of children.

War is not healthy for children and other living things. Maybe we should just leave it at that, but we cannot do so. It is too easy for us to mouth the words, to recall the slogan, and then pass on to business as usual. We found that although we had heard and said those words many times they had not really registered with us. We had to open ourselves to the experience of real war. Real war is neither the fantasies we dream of when we hear patriotic speeches nor the pretend games we engaged in as children when we played war. Real war is the end of childhood.

Real War Is Not for Children

This is modern war as children experience it:

> At first, it was just a morbid whistling overhead, the sound of an antipersonnel rocket in the dying moments of flight. Then it exploded in a shattering burst of smoke and dust. A group of children had been playing a noisy game of tag near their mud-walled homes. Now, as the smoke cleared on this bright December afternoon, there was only moaning. Near the crater dug by the rocket lay two children, a boy of

17 and his 6-year-old sister, shattered by shards of twisted steel. Around them nearly a dozen other children were strewn about, many of them grievously wounded. . . . It took 20 minutes for any help to appear. By then, another youngster, a 4-year-old girl, had died. By dusk, three more children were dead. (Burns 1990)

Good tactics, these antipersonnel rockets: they wound many more than they kill and thus tie up a lot of resources (not to mention exert a demoralizing force by providing living reminders of the opponent's insistent presence).

War is more than its essential killing and maiming, however. It is also a social and economic force in the life of a society. It can have dramatic demographic implications. Because of World War II a young man is sent to England as an American soldier and meets a young woman who had volunteered to serve in the British Air Force. They marry and a new international alliance is forged. Untold thousands of African-Americans moved north to work in factories born of the war economy in both World War I and World War II, and that experience, coupled with the military service of a generation of African-American men, altered their consciousness and the future history of the nation.

In the United States only the South has experienced the fire storm of being a war zone, and that was more than 125 years ago. In the United States war has meant economic boom times. But for most of the world, war means economic decline, even disaster. Particularly in countries where the economy struggles to meet basic human needs even in the best of times, war often means economic catastrophe. In Africa, for example, wars in the last three decades have meant famine for millions. In Central and South America war means malnutrition and an intensification of poverty for people already living on the economic edge. All these social threats combine with the basic psychological threats to make living in a war zone an attack on childhood, because peace is fundamental to the very meaning of childhood.

What Does It Mean to Be a Child?

What does it mean to be a child? Children are not short adults. They come to us with capabilities and needs that we must nurture and support before they can become adults. Childhood is the process through which the human organism becomes the complete human person. Part of this process derives from human biology.

Children are born with a drive to become attached to parents and others in their social environment, and they come equipped with what it will take to make that connection. They can learn to identify familiar faces, voices, and smells. And they can respond to those familiar people with friendly looks and sounds, and eventually with smiles of recognition. Attachment is perhaps the most important item on the child's developmental agenda in the first year of life. Erik Erikson (1963) identified the development of this "basic trust" as the most important challenge during the first year of life. Armed with basic trust the child is ready to face the world secure in the knowledge that people are caring and the world is trustworthy.

In the second and third years of life the child confronts other challenges. If given support and guidance by parents and others, the child becomes more and more competent. This growing competence means the child is ever more ready emotionally and intellectually to face the next challenge, and to do so with confidence, with joy, and with love. To live a complete life one must learn to love, to work, and to play. To play?

Play figures prominently in what it means to be a child. That much is a biological given. But it has taken cultural evolution to provide social support for the full flowering of that innate capacity. In the modern sense, childhood is a special period in the life course when we shield the individual from the direct demands of the economic, sexual, and political forces of the adult world. Children are not short adults.

As a concept, "childhood" is one of the major accomplishments of the modern era. The United Nations recognized this truth in 1989 with passage of the Convention on the Rights of the Child, an effort to institutionalize the concept of childhood in international law. Unlike adults who are expected to earn their own keep and pay their own way, modern children have an absolute economic claim on us. If their parents cannot provide for them, the local, state, national, or international community has an obligation to care for them.

Children are also exempt from adult sexuality. Their need for physical affection, their need for attachment, their need for intimacy, are all to be encouraged in a nonsexual way—at least so far as adults are concerned. As sociologist David Finkelhor (1984) so aptly puts it, children cannot give informed consent for sex with adults. To give informed consent an individual must understand the potential consequences of an action *and* be free to say yes or no. We take it as a given that children can meet neither of these conditions when it comes to adult sexuality. They can not fully appreciate what it means (for them now and in the future), nor do they have the autonomy vis à vis adults to say no. The presumption of adult dominance and authority in any adult-child encounter rules this out.

And finally, the modern concept of childhood reflects the idea that children are not full participants in the world of adult politics. They cannot vote, are not legally responsible, and are not to be used as political pawns by competing adult political forces in their society. They are not expected to serve in the armed forces. One of the most hotly debated features of the UN Convention on the Rights of the Child concerns the age at which military service should begin—as a compromise, the convention says "fifteen years old," but many countries argued for eighteen.

More broadly, we expect children to relate to adults on a direct person-to-person basis in which *who* you are matters more than *what* you do. We do not expect children to operate in the organized bureaucratic way in which adults must relate to each other—at least some of the time.

And we have a different conception of "responsibility" for children. A child's parents are responsible for what the child does. We recognize that children who do bad things merit special treatment. They are in a different class. It is partly for this reason that the UN Convention on the Rights of the Child prohibits the death penalty for children under eighteen. Although most nations of the world subscribed to this distinction, the government of the United States resisted signing the convention because we as a country reserve the right to execute children (and are almost alone in the world in doing so) (Cohen and Davidson 1990).

But if the child is shielded from economic, sexual, and political forces, what then is childhood all about? Play! Children have a license to play, and in so doing they explore the world. This play is distinguished from adult work in that it does not depend upon formal organizations and is not aimed at production for its justification. It differs from adult social life in that it is not the basis for courtship.

This "free" play is fundamentally human, and from it comes the best that humanity has to offer. Play is the key to the "long childhood" that Jacob Bronowski (1973) and others have rightly identified as the key to human cultural evolution. Moreover, play is inextricably linked to the development of competence in childhood. Language and thought arise from the playful interactions of child and parents, child and siblings, child and others. Through play children learn the ropes of their culture and wrestle with the emotional and intellectual challenges they encounter. Children play and in so doing develop the basis for competence in adulthood—competence in all its many senses: intellectual, emotional, and physical. Children with any shred of childhood left to them play, and they play at what they know.

In the West Bank's Jalazon refugee camp Palestinian children play the game of *Intifada*. The children playing the part of Palestinian demonstrators gather stones to throw at the children playing the part of Israeli soldiers. The soldiers then charge the demonstrators, hitting them with sticks, "firing" tear gas canisters, and shooting them with stick guns. Sometimes children really do get hurt when they are hit with a stone or poked with a stick. All this when in the real world more than 50,000 children—about 1 in every 20 Palestinian children—have been seriously injured in the real-life "limited war" in which they live.

Robert is a ten-year-old living in a public housing project in Chicago. One day while he was playing outside in the vacant lot next to the project he became an urban war zone casualty. His uncle, who was nearby, reports that the boy was running after a friend in a game of tag, and then the next thing he knew Robert was down on the ground, clutching his neck, gasping for breath. A bullet fired from a speeding car, aimed at a rival gang's headquarters, had gone astray. Robert became part of the body count in Chicago.

Chicago? Yes, even in a society officially "at peace," some children live in war zones. The War on Drugs. The War *of* Drugs. The War on Ourselves. Southside of Chicago: 25 percent of the kids have witnessed a murder by the time they are seventeen (Bell 1989). "Serious assaults" have increased 400 percent since the mid-1970s. Nearly 100 percent of the children have had firsthand encounters with shooting: someone is shot, bullets come through windows, people avoid going outside for fear of getting shot. The children in a nursery school regularly play a game called "funeral," in which children take turns being the corpse, while others reenact the mourning of relatives, friends, and neighbors for the loss of a child to gunfire or knives.

Living with the Danger of Just Being Who You Are

Living in a war zone means living with danger, the chronic threat of violent assault, assault that is not a function of who you are as an individual. This differentiates living in a war zone for a child from the experience of child abuse, where violence arises in the context of a specific interpersonal relationship. At its worst, child abuse means the relationships closest to the heart of children are turned against them. While war may be related to child abuse, it is not the same.

In a war zone, you and the ones you love are the target of assault because of group affiliation and social identity. You are in jeopardy just because you are who you are when you happen to be the wrong person in the wrong place at the wrong time—all of the time.

CAMBODIA. A nine-year-old boy joins his mother in a trip into the forest outside his village in search of food. His village is very poor, and his family must augment their meager diet of rice with what edible berries they can find in the woods. A land mine buried in the path explodes when the boy steps on it. He survives the explosion but loses his leg. It will be more than a year before his name comes up on the list to receive assistance in obtaining a prosthesis.

PALESTINE. A ten-year-old girl is on her way to buy milk for her mother. While passing through the town square she is hit in the stomach by a bullet fired by a soldier firing at a group of rock-throwing youth. A boy is sitting in his yard with his family eating supper when a grenade explodes. He is blinded and loses both his legs and one of his arms. A little Israeli girl on her way home to her West Bank settlement from a family gathering is critically injured when a rock thrown by a demonstrator smashes the window of her parents' car.

CHICAGO. An eight-year-old boy emerging from his school is shot in the head. The bullet was fired by a teenage gang member at another gang's leader. It misses the gang leader but hits the eight-year-old as he walks by the scene. In another incident, a thirteen-year-old is killed when a bullet fired by gang members comes through his apartment window and finds him sitting on the couch in the living room.

We know that children die in war zones. We began with a recent report by UNICEF (1986) estimating that whereas in earlier times the nature of war meant that military personnel constituted most of the casualties, in recent times that situation has been reversed. In today's wars, with their emphasis on "national liberation," "counterinsurgency," "low-intensity conflict," and "guerilla warfare," more than 80 percent of the direct and indirect victims of military action are children and women.

The changing technology of warfare has contributed to this trend. Antipersonnel mines, shells, rubber bullets, rockets, carpet bombing, automatic weapons, and the other products of modern weapons development make the carnage harder to contain, more difficult to limit to armed combatants, even if you wish to do so. Many do not.

Indeed, systematic attacks on civilians, including children, have become the norm rather than the exception. Many, if not most, of the children killed in warfare today are not *individually* targeted. But attacks on civilian centers—towns, villages, and cities—mean death and injury to children.

We know that children die in war zones. But how do children *live* in war zones? How do they cope? How do they adapt? And at what cost to their minds and spirits? These are the questions we have sought to answer. We have looked to research conducted over the last fifty years by clinicians and others concerned with children. And we have looked for answers in our own conversations with children and adults in war zones around the world.

Through our personal journey we have found that war transforms the personal and collective life of a people, as it transformed us. War moves people and ideas, as we were moved. It stimulates technological innovation and shakes up society, and we were shaken by our experiences. It causes people to think and feel and see and hear what they might never even have imagined, and we have come to see things in a new light. General George Patton is purported to have observed that "compared with war all other forms of human activity pale into insignificance." But at what cost?

2

At What Cost?

Children who live through war and other forms of social crisis may adapt in ways that produce impaired development, physical damage, and emotional trauma. What is more, these children may be missocialized into a model of fear, violence, and hatred. For many children, war is a crucible of darkness from which they emerge bitter, angry, and distrustful. They may learn all too well the primal lesson of war: kill and/or be killed. No one learns this terrible lesson better than children who are *forced* to fight against their own people. Children in Mozambique are kidnapped by antigovernment bandits and compelled to join their "army" under the threat of death if they refuse. Once conscripted, these children are subjected to intensive brutalization and indoctrination to prepare them to accept orders to kill. In Cambodia, too, the Khmer Rouge impressed children into service and forced them to become executioners.

But not all children who serve as soldiers are conscripted by force. In the Middle East, Palestinian children and youth have been in the vanguard of confrontations between Palestinians and Israeli soldiers and police. Most of these young people are volunteers. Pasternak's Dr. Zhivago tells us that "happy men do not volunteer" to fight, and we might add that happy children do not rush to risk their lives in battle.

Teenagers do volunteer to fight, particularly if they see fighting as a way to achieve status and prestige, with peers and adults. They also volunteer if they are angry, if they despair of a better future, or if they believe in a cause. There are always adults ready to offer making war as a way for adolescents to find themselves. It is often said that "old men make wars; young men fight them." There is much truth to this. In today's world the consequences of this truth is that millions of children must contend with the extreme challenges to development posed by living in a war zone.

What Does War Do to and for Children?

For teenagers, war may offer a chance to move forward in identity and status, to escape dead ends at home, or just to feel the excitement of change and challenge. But for children the story is quite different. War kills children. It maims children. It injures children. But when war touches young children, the greatest single threat they face is the disruption of attachment relationships.

Among the traumatic experiences children face during wartime are loss of home, separation from family members, and the violent death of a parent or family member. The first concern of a young child is to maintain the primary relationships of life. If children can achieve that much, they have a good chance of staying on track developmentally.

The child's understanding of the world is very concrete. For a child, it is *my* house, *my* parents, *my* sisters, *my* brothers, *my* grandmother, *my* grandfather, *my* aunts, *my* uncles, *my* cousins, *my* toys, *my* pets. If that much remains intact, the child is rich in the most important ways in which a child can be rich. Anna Freud's reports on children exposed to trauma during World War II offered some of the earliest professional accounts of this basic reality (Freud and Burlingham 1943). She found that children who live in the midst of bombardment but in the care of their own mothers or of familiar mother substitutes were not psychologically devastated by wartime experiences. If parents could maintain day-to-day care routines *and* project high morale, their children had a foundation of basic trust from which to build as they sought to cope with the stresses around them.

A similar theme emerges from our recent study of safety issues for children in a public housing project in Chicago that is saturated with violence. Mothers in the project identified "shooting" as their major safety concern for their children. But by utilizing a variety of coping mechanisms to project a feeling of safety to their children, their children seemed to be able to survive. This is not to say that such children escaped unscathed, however. Adjusting to the challenge of living with chronic violence can be emotionally exhausting. And many children and mothers living in the world's war zones are exhausted.

The eventual consequences of early traumatic loss may not be fully evident until many years have passed. A study of Dutch resistance fighters in World War II found that for some it was decades before the psychic toll of what they had experienced was fully felt (van der Kolk 1987). Some of the children studied by Anna Freud who had lost their parents during World War II but had received compensatory care and treatment revealed significant chronic and profound problems in adulthood. Recent long-term studies of the impact of divorce on children conducted by J. Wallerstein and S. Blakeslee (1989) suggest a similar "sleeper effect," with life adjustment problems emerging ten or more years after the fact of family dissolution. It may take years to see the full consequences of a childhood spent in a war zone. But why do some children cope better than others?

Who Copes? Why?

When we look at research done in an effort to understand why some children overcome difficult life circumstances, several important themes emerge. Factors that lead to pro-social behavior and healthy adaptability in the face of stressful early experience include a series of ameliorating factors (Lösel and Bliesener 1990):

ACTIVELY TRYING TO COPE WITH STRESS (rather than just reacting) and temperamental characteristics that favor active coping attempts and positive relationships with others (e.g., activity, goal orientation, sociability) rather than passive withdrawal.

Even in a war situation there is something to be done. Those who become demoralized and give up increase their psychological vulnerability. Those who continue to struggle to make sense of the world, whether children or the adults who care for children, are more resilient. We recognize that some children are born more active and outgoing than others. These temperamental differences matter. Indeed, many studies have found that "attractive" children who succeed in difficult circumstances often seem to have an uncanny knack for finding and drawing to themselves the social and personal resources they need. But children can learn this active coping style.

COGNITIVE COMPETENCE (at least an average level of intelligence).

Being smart helps. Intelligence means the ability to figure things out, to read situations and people, to create alternatives. For a child faced with living in a war zone, every ounce of intelligence increases the odds of survival. What is more, this same intelligence helps shield the child from simplistic interpretations of experience that are self-defeating and socially destructive in the long run.

EXPERIENCES OF SELF-EFFICACY and a corresponding self-confidence and positive self-esteem.

War zones carry with them a pervasive corrosion of self. The child needs all the reservoirs of self-esteem possible. Building this positive sense of self is an investment in resilience.

A STABLE EMOTIONAL RELATIONSHIP with at least one parent or other reference person.

Child development is a partnership; children cannot develop properly alone. Perhaps the single most important resource a child can have for dealing with difficult circumstances is a strong, positive attachment with someone who is "crazy about" that child. This is why children who lose their parents *after* they have established a strong relationship with them have something to work with if given an opportunity to form new replacement relationships. Research on children growing up in war zones tells us that children who have experienced a warm, positive relationship with parents can develop a "working model" of what it means to be a person that can serve to sustain them through hard times. Parents and the quality of their relationships with their children are a key to understanding the psychological health of children who live in war zones.

AN OPEN, SUPPORTIVE EDUCATIONAL CLIMATE and parental models of behavior that encourage constructive coping with problems.

Particularly as the child grows into later childhood and adolescence, it is crucial that the child be exposed to a social environment that sponsors and encourages a process of interpretation. A child growing up in difficult circumstances needs help in "processing" those experiences. The child needs an education that helps to show the path to a moral universe in which the child himself or herself can participate.

SOCIAL SUPPORT FROM PERSONS OUTSIDE THE FAMILY.

The child is not just part of a family. The child is part of a community. We forget this vital truth at our peril. Even the most basic of developmental phenomena have a community component. Whether it be intelligence or moral judgment, the tone set by the community, and the concrete ways in which it offers the child (and the child's parents) nurturance and guidance, can play a critical role in how the child develops, in who he or she becomes. In the simplest sense, the community is crucial in offering orphaned and abandoned children a second chance through adoption and foster care, particularly if those new relationships provide children with a chance to "process" their loss of parents.

These factors have been identified as important when the stresses involved are in the "normal" range found in the mainstream of modern industrial societies: poverty, family conflict, childhood physical disability, and parental involvement in substance abuse. Nonetheless, they may provide a starting point for efforts to understand the special character of coping in the stressful circumstances of war where the risk of socially maladaptive coping is high.

If we use conclusions developed in the limited situations studied by most researchers and apply them to a war situation, we can understand why some children manage to cope while others do not, and even why some children accept the moral challenge of living with violence and rise to the occasion. Successful children bring to the situation of war a developmental track record of competence. They bring a positive orientation to the world. They bring a supportive network of relationships. These are children who have positive momentum in their lives.

Beyond any individual strengths that come to a child with temperament and intellectual capacity at birth, the key lies in the balance of social supports from and for parents. It lies in parental capacity to buffer social stress in the lives of children and offer them a positive path to follow in dealing with that stress. The quality of life for young children—and their reservoirs of resilience—thus becomes a *social* indicator as well as a measure of personal worth. This hypothesis emerges from a wide range of research and clinical observation.

It finds validation in studies conducted in World War II that conclude that the level of emotional upset displayed by adults in a child's life, not the war situation itself, was the most important factor in predicting the child's response (Freud and Burlingham 1943). Assessments of the impact of bombing raids on children in London during World War II gave rise to this hypothesis; our own observations tend to confirm it. Children who live with positive adults can usually cope, even with major stress; children who live with frightened and demoralized adults can be overcome by much lower levels of stress.

This is not to say that children will be invulnerable to trauma if we simply ensure that they remain in the care of positive-thinking adults and everyone remains calm. Some experiences are so awful that even socially and emotionally supported children may be pushed to and beyond their limit. This is the basis for a category of response labeled post traumatic stress disorder (PTSD).

Developed by psychiatrists and other mental health professionals, the concept of PTSD refers to stresses that are "outside the range of human experience" (i.e., that are abnormally intense). It is reasonable to expect symptoms of distress in most psychologically normal people. The symptoms include intrusive ideas and feelings about the precipitating event, denial and emotional numbing, excessive sensitivity to stimuli associated with the trauma, and diminished expectations for the future. Together, these defining characteristics point our attention to horrible things that can happen to children under extraordinary circumstances, and teach us to appreciate that what may at first appear to be bizarre behaviors on the part of children are simply responses that are normal for children who are afflicted with traumatic experiences. Most of the research and clinical practice underlying our understanding of PTSD in children addresses acute, traumatic events.

But these criteria also raise the question of how to understand the behavior of children for whom horror is not an event that disrupts the normal flow of daily life, but a condition of that life, for whom there is no "post" trauma period, whose whole life *is* the trauma. These are the children in whom we are most interested, the children of war, for whom what is ordinarily "outside the range of human experience" becomes the day-to-day. We fear for these children, for theirs is not simply the emotional challenge of "getting over" a horrible experience. Theirs is the task of finding a way to make sense of a world in which horrible experiences become part of the fabric of life and for whom *Chronic* Traumatic Stress Disorder is the problem.

For these children the task goes beyond "simply" overcoming the symptoms of PTSD. They may well experience PTSD. One study of children who lived through the hell of Cambodia under the Khmer Rouge reports that 50 percent were manifesting symptoms of PTSD four years later (Kinzie et al. 1986). Another reports that more than half the children of Lebanon affected by the Israeli invasion in 1982 were suffering from psychosomatic symptoms four years later (Rayhida, Shaya, and Armenian 1986). But even this is not the whole story. There remains the task of making cosmic sense of the experience, making sense of a dangerous world.

Making Sense of a Dangerous World: The Role of Ideology

Human beings are "meaning-seeking organisms." We try to find meaning in our experience. Without meaning we tend to get lost and succumb to self-destructive or antisocial behavior or to madness. One important way we develop a sense of meaningfulness in our lives is by formulating personal and collective narratives, stories that explain and integrate experience. Psychologists are beginning to understand the importance of these personal and collective narratives for mental health.

One source of mental health is a compelling and consistent story that bolsters the individual's sense of self-worth, that offers a basically comprehensible picture of the world, and that lays out a path to the future. One aspect of narrative that enables children to survive emotionally in the midst of war-induced trauma is ideological, offering a worldview that makes sense of experience in political, religious, and social terms.

But at what cost? The same narrative that interprets the child's experience and its relation to the larger world beyond the family may set in motion the dark forces of the human spirit. It may make sense of the world through hatred and negativism. The same ideology that gives meaning to life in a war zone may also lead to a process of dehumanization ("What the enemy does is less than human") and demonization ("The enemy are devils").

Dehumanization and demonization may prolong the conflict by reducing the possibility of compromise and by training children to seek destruction of their enemies as the path to emotional survival and personal integration. Too many of the world's conflicts reveal this terrible circular dynamic. Children manage to cope with the trauma of war by holding fast to an ideology that explains and justifies their lives, but when they grow up this same ideology spurs them to continue the war and subject another generation of children to suffering.

Human rights groups that have studied the life histories of professional torturers find that many are the result of a "training program" in which youth are themselves brutalized and tortured. This desensitizes them to brutality *and* teaches the important lesson that "anything is possible; nothing is prohibited." Once this lesson is learned, the torturers are taught that their enemies are subhuman and/or demonic. Thus the torturers come to believe that they can commit any atrocity against the enemy because enemy lives have no value.

These two lessons together prepare the individual to inflict the most heinous torture without remorse. There is no shortage of torturers in the world, and no limits to what they will do. In Chile and elsewhere in Latin America, during the various counterinsurgency operations (e.g., Argentina's "Dirty War" against progressive and revolutionary political elements) it has been common to torture children in front of their parents to intimidate those parents and force them to bend to the will of the authorities. This is a special kind of "war against children," the effects of which are almost too painful to recount. When the enemy is beyond human bounds, there are no boundaries in respect in what you do. Ideology can aid and abet that process.

Ideology is the public expression of a person's inner moral map of the world, a person's phenomenology. As a worldview, ideology figures prominently in successful coping under conditions of extreme danger (Garbarino and Associates 1982). Many observers have pointed to the importance of ideological factors in sustaining the ability to function under extreme stress. In his observations about life in Nazi concentration camps, Bruno Bettelheim (1943) noted that those who bore up best were those with intense ideological commitments (most notably the ultrareligious and the Communists), commitments that offered meaning impervious to day-to-day brutalization. Among inner-city black Americans living in a racist society, and contending with crime-plagued environments, fundamentalist religious groups that offer a political ideology (e.g., the Black Muslims) may serve the same function.

In the Israeli-Palestinian conflict in the Gaza Strip and West Bank, Moslem fundamentalist groups (such as the Hamas) play this role for Palestinians. As the conflict over the political future of the Palestinians dragged on through the late 1980s and into the early 1990s Islamic extremists found an ever more fertile climate for their ideology. Kill the Israelis, they argued, because it is a noble religious mission to do so. The path to heaven is open to those who die in this cause.

Extreme Zionist groups serve the same function and offer essentially the same message for Jewish Israelis. By simplifying what is an extremely complex human conflict, extreme Zionism offers a peculiar "peace of mind" to those who accept it. A study in Israel reports that ultra-Orthodox Jews suffer less stress as a result of the Palestinian uprising than more secular Jews (Pines 1989). The former tend to see the issue in simplistic ideological terms (e.g., as a necessary prelude to fulfilling their Zionist dream of "Greater Israel"). The latter suffer from the stress of being battered by their consciences as they seek to balance competing loyalties and values (their commitment to a democratic ethic, the ethical imperatives of Judaism and their Zionist vision, and their fears and hopes for national security). Religious fanatics (and secular political extremists) always have an easier time, in the sense of living without the doubts that come with openness, empathy, honesty, and an appreciation for the complexity of real-life conflicts.

Hundreds of Israeli soldiers have refused on grounds of conscience to participate in the military/police activities involved in combating the Palestinian uprising in the West Bank and Gaza Strip. Other Israelis risk harassment, ostracism, and bodily harm for articulating a political solution that embraces Palestinian national self-determination. Israelis who are conscience-stricken by the problems of the Palestinians and who demonstrate their beliefs through political protests are spat upon and attacked by right-wing zealots.

On the other side of the conflict, Palestinian Islamic fundamentalists take comfort in *their* extremist ideology, which promises an end to the state of Israel and the return to the Palestinians of lands taken by the Israelis in 1948 and in 1967. Meanwhile, democratic-humanistic Palestinians must contend with the stressful moral ambiguities they face as they seek ethically acceptable ways to participate in the nationalist struggle, a struggle that forces them to find a path that acknowledges the historical and moral claims of the Zionists while asserting the national rights of Palestinians in an ethically tenable fashion in the face of overwhelming military power. They too face personal threats, including the constant reminder that they may face injury or death for being labeled a "collaborator." Since the *Intifada* began, one Palestinian "collaborator" has been killed by fellow Palestinians for every three Palestinians killed by the Israelis.

Thus, stress (even moral tension) is the *necessary* price one pays for moral sensibility in the midst of extreme conflict. American reformer Myles Horton put it this way:

> I was told one time during an educational conference that I was cruel because I made people who were very happy and contented unhappy, and that it was wrong to upset people and stretch their imaginations and minds and to challenge them to the place where they got themselves in trouble, became maladjusted, and so on. I think that people aren't fully free until they're in a struggle for justice. And this means for everyone. It's a struggle of such importance that they are willing, if necessary, to die for it. I think that's what you have to do before you're really free. Then you've got something to live for. You don't want to die, because you've got so much you want to do. This struggle is so important that it gives a meaning to life. (Horton 1990, 42)

Ideology is an important psychological resource. But unless it refuses to accept dehumanization and demonization of the enemy, the more powerful the ideology is as a psychological resource, the more it serves to truncate moral development. In this sense, it may become a serious impediment to political settlement.

The strong commitment of American Southerners to their cause prolonged the Civil War well beyond the time when there was any reasonable chance of victory. The Nazi ideology of Hitler and his supporters caused them to expose Germany to the risk of total destruction. Ideology sustains bravery and persistence, which in the service of an evil cause, such as slavery or anti-Semitism, means needless suffering and death. There is no simple accounting for the implications of belief.

Children and Ideology

This is our adult perspective, of course. Children can participate in ideology directly, but with the limitations imposed by their concrete intellectual orientation and their concern for firsthand relationships. What matters is what kind of ideology appeals to the child (and is appealing to the child). For children, ideology is mainly a matter of compelling stories that relate the child's personal experiences to experiences in the community and to the future.

Beyond songs and slogans, ideology may motivate and rationalize active participation by children in war-related struggles. For example, children carried weapons and explosive devices on behalf of the Viet Cong's nationalist cause in Vietnam. Palestinian children and youth serve in the front lines in their nationalist struggle. In Iran children and youth became cannon fodder to please Ayatollah Khomeini.

In Nazi Germany youthful ideologues sustained the war effort— and in the final stages of World War II took their places to die before the Allied armies, as had Southern youth before them in the final stages of the American Civil War. Israeli youth have been on the front lines of Zionism for generations—living in communities in disputed areas, sometimes under fire by the armies of hostile neighbors, always subject to terrorist attacks.

The importance of the ideological dimension emerges repeatedly in accounts of families under stress. Political and religious interpretation can play an important role in shaping the consequences of experience, particularly when they are held to with "fanatic" intensity—and fanatical adherence to an ideology is often necessary as a defense against the crushing weight of reality in a concentration camp, a prison, or a refugee camp.

Researcher Raija-Leena Punamaki saw this process at work in the case of Palestinians living in refugee camps and under Israeli occupation, where every feature of day-to-day stress and physical deprivation is met with a process of ideological response that mobilizes social and psychological resources:

> The psychological processes of healing the traumatic experiences drew strength from political and ideological commitment. Nationalistic motivation was present at all stages of the stress process. The meaning

and harmfulness of an event as well as sufficiency of one's own resources to cope with stressors were approached in the wider social and political context of a victimized and struggling nation. (Punamaki 1987, 82–83)

The fact that war danger can lead to emotional trauma, developmental impairment, and extremist, revenge-oriented ideology is not the whole story, however. Ideology need not be simplistic, extremist, and dehumanizing. A second theme in studies of the children of war emphasizes the role of social crisis in stimulating enhanced moral development. For example, in his study of the political life of children, psychiatrist Robert Coles noted that under conditions of violent political crisis *some* children develop a precocious and precious moral sensibility. On the one hand, we have the commonsense assumption that children exposed to danger are destined for developmental difficulties: war is not good for children and other living things. On the other hand, we have the fact that children survive such danger and may even overcome its challenges in ways that enhance development.

They may come through the challenge of facing danger with an enhanced capacity to see the world with sensitivity and moral astuteness. This can happen if adults help them process their experiences, heal their pain, and help put those painful experiences in a humanistic framework that refuses to dehumanize the enemy and instead encourages the development of empathy.

The Israeli son of a thrice-decorated veteran of four wars speaks up for the human and political rights of Palestinians and is beaten up by his schoolmates. An eight-year-old Jewish girl living in an Israeli settlement in the West Bank observes a group of Palestinian children being detained by Israeli soldiers. Her own father serves as a soldier in the reserves. She is upset at the prospect of children being hurt by her father, even though she understands that the children throw rocks at soldiers. She demands reassurance from him that he would not hurt any children even if they were "misbehaving." These children show us some of the best.

Perhaps even more powerful is the moral testimony of a ten-year-old Palestinian girl we interviewed in the refugee camp where her family has lived since 1948. She opposes the Israeli occupation, and she participates in demonstrations. When asked to draw a picture of "where she lives and what it is like to live there," she drew a picture that incorporated demonstrations, soldiers, roadblocks, and tear gas. This is the reality of her life: a war, albeit a "limited war."

After her school was closed, teachers held informal classes in their homes and in other buildings until they were told by the Israeli authorities that such classes were prohibited and they faced arrest and demolition of their homes if they persisted. So this girl started holding classes for the younger children on the sly.

She has a clear political consciousness and participates in the uprising—even to the point of composing nationalist songs. She is involved in confronting the soldiers and has seen children hurt by soldiers. But her father is a teacher, and she is a bright child with a natural gift for analysis. When asked how the soldiers treated their own children when they are at home, she replied, "They treat them normally as a father should, but they do this here to us because this is their orders." When asked what she felt about the soldiers, she told us how the soldiers have come into her home at night many times, and that this frightened her younger brothers and sisters.

We asked her what she does then, and she said that she calms and comforts "the little ones." "How?" we asked. Her answer: "I tell the children that the soldiers are human beings just like us." We are humbled by such a display of fundamental empathy.

Children like this little girl and her Israeli counterparts represent a precious resource, as do their "cousins" in Nicaragua, Mozambique, Cambodia, and Chicago. Amidst a tendency on both sides to project a rigid dehumanization and demonization of "the enemy," they have been helped to hold on to a sense of human connection, of empathy. That there are reserves of humanism among children living in political violence and chronic conflict, and that they can speak with an advanced moral voice, is a good sign. Amidst all the darkness—and there is so much darkness—there are glimmers of light.

Finding these glimmers and nurturing them depends upon being able to hear what children and youth are telling us about their efforts to cope with the consequences of living in danger. What can children tell us about living in a war zone?

What Children Can Tell Us?

What children can tell us depends on what we as adults are prepared to hear (Garbarino, Stott, and Erikson Institute 1989). We mean "prepared" here in two senses. It means being motivated to hear, wanting to hear, being willing to listen to children express their pain. And it means being willing to hear children struggle with the confusion that comes when one must make sense of what fundamentally does *not* make sense.

We have trained ourselves to listen and to hear. We have come to understand how difficult true listening is for us as adults, as American adults. We naturally want to feel reassured that we are on the right side. This need is particularly strong among Americans, and we often become desperately angry when told we are not on the right side. Being right and good is more important to Americans than anything else in our national character.

Some of the viciousness of America's policies toward conflicts around the world stem from this need. When we are not accepted as "the good guys," when our self-defined helpfulness is rejected, when "they" do not do what we believe to be the right thing, we become enraged and capable of horrible things. The merciless bombing of our enemies in Southeast Asia and our campaign against the Sandinistas are but two examples of our sometimes barbarous actions.

As individuals we want to believe that the world is just and sensible. We want to hear in what children tell us that those who have been hurt somehow deserved their pain. One way to do this is to define the people whom we hurt as "Communists," or "terrorists," or "savages," or "rebels."

To really hear the children of war we found it necessary to approach them first not as Communist children or Sandinista children or Contra children or Zionist children or PLO children or rebel children or government children, but as children. Of course, to appreciate fully their identities we must recognize their cultural, national, and ideological voices.

These voices are often an important part of their story. But to really hear the children we must learn to listen to them without labels. Having heard them as simply children we can then interpret them with the aid of all those labels. But first, we must simply listen to the children.

Most of the children exposed to significant trauma can survive and overcome it if they have the support of parents, or of someone else who cares for them and loves them if parents are unavailable. What percent achieve this? In most cases it appears the clear majority, perhaps as many as 85 percent, will overcome their symptoms of distress and will find a way to live a "normal" life (Fish-Murray 1990).

These "overcomers" don't forget, and they are changed—forever. And if things are unusually horrible—such as the "killing fields" of Cambodia—the proportion who overcome the trauma may decrease and even become a minority. Who they become if they survive is a question for us to answer as adults. Will they get the supportive treatment they need? Will they find a safe place to heal? Will the most seriously hurt ones have access to healing therapy? Will their stories be told and listened to in a way that helps them make sense of the world? Are we ready to listen to the children of war zones?

3

Cambodian Survivors:

Hell Is a Time and Place

The young man is introduced as cochairman of Youth for Peace, an international group of young people who travel the world talking about war and making a plea for peace. Arn Chorn is Khmer, a Cambodian, and he tells us his story of innocence lost under Pol Pot's Khmer Rouge in the period 1975–79. He recounts his experiences as a child after the Khmer Rouge took over in his native country and Pol Pot's faction became preeminent: it is a story of torment and suffering. As a child he witnessed the brutal killing of family and friends. He was forced to participate in acts of barbarism—killing people who broke the arbitrary rules or who just happened to offend the twisted sensibilities of the Khmer Rouge authorities.

His story is terrible enough to hear; one can only imagine what it was like to live. Evidence has been accumulating in the work of psychologists dealing with Cambodian refugees in the United States of just how hard it was. Substantial numbers of Cambodians who witnessed the horror of the Khmer Rouge have gone blind, perhaps as a way of coping.

One account, written for a professional journal serving psychologists, offers the following report:

A woman watched her 3-month-old nephew being beaten to death against a tree by members of Pol Pot's army, the Khmer Rouge. Soon after, she saw her brother's other three children clubbed to death. Then, while working in a field near her home, she saw her brother—a police officer for the deposed leader Lon Nol—and his wife assassinated by the Khmer Rouge some 100 feet in front of her. Soon after witnessing these events, her vision started to deteriorate. (DeAngelis 1990)

She is not alone; research indicates that many Cambodian women who lived through the hell of the Khmer Rouge have responded in a similar fashion. One Cambodian woman reported simply, "My family was killed in 1975, and I cried for four years. When I stopped crying, I was blind" (DeAngelis 1990).

Blindness is a horrible price to pay for witnessing such horror. These victims seem to be saying that they have seen enough. Perhaps deep down they feel so guilty about being survivors that they feel the need to be punished. No one knows for sure. We just know that the phenomenon is real.

Surviving something like the Khmer Rouge holocaust was a matter of persistence coupled with good fortune for most of those who did survive. One survivor with whom we have spoken recounted how fighting near his forced labor camp offered him and the other prisoners a chance for liberation. Some prisoners ran to the right and escaped; others ran to the left and were killed in the cross fire. Why did he run to the right? "I can't remember," he says, "I was just lucky."

As Arn Chorn speaks, his placid demeanor changes and his tears begin to flow as he recalls memories of what the Khmer Rouge did and of what he did. Most of those in the audience of five hundred professionals attending the conference on children and war are stunned by Arn Chorn's story. Even many of those who knew what to expect are stunned.

Here is a soul tormented more than a decade later by events of grotesquely naked aggression against children, against the very fabric of childhood as we understand it. He ends with a plea for peace. His message haunts us still, and we think of him often as we ourselves make the trip to Southeast Asia in search of his past.

A Tower of Skulls

We think of Arn Chorn five months later as we stand at the site of one of the "killing fields" in Cambodia. A short drive from the capital city of Phnom Penh, these few acres hold the remains of approximately 20,000 men, women, and children. They were killed systematically by Pol Pot's Khmer Rouge government between 1975 and 1979, and buried here in mass graves. Here to our right is a tree. It was used as a tool for killing infants: they were swung by their feet and their heads were smashed against its trunk. This method was very effective—it rarely required more than two tries to kill a victim.

Ahead of us is a hole thirty feet by twenty-five feet in which were found the remains of 106 children. It is one of dozens of such grisly excavations at this one site. Each hole holds the remains of a specialized slaughter or the result of a particular day's or week's killing. Thousands of skulls are piled together in a macabre monument at the center of the field. Some skulls are grouped by category: "children between the ages of seven and fifteen" says one identifying sign, "children under the age of seven" says another. The shelves of skulls stretch upward to the height of a four-story building. Many unexcavated graves lie beyond the nearby fence: "Too much danger of disease to risk exposing them," we are told.

We walk among the death pits with a Cambodian man of our own generation. A soft-spoken man with warmth and intelligence showing in his eyes, he was a young man during the Pol Pot years: his parents and all four of his brothers and sisters perished in the holocaust of 1975–79. The rain has exposed a human leg bone so that it emerges from the side of one of the grave sites. He pulls it out and throws it back into the pit where it disappears beneath the dirty water that has accumulated there. This killing field is a fundamental accusation, a profound statement about what is possible when humanity's dark side becomes dominant.

The field with its death pits and its tower of skulls is an exercise in "propaganda," to be sure. It has been partially excavated and publicized as a way of distancing the present government from what went before (even though some of those who were part of *that* government are now part of *this* government). It is a statement that serves the political needs of the government now in power. But it is more than that. This tower of skulls, like the memorials at Auschwitz, is an indictment against every human being because fellow members of our species have done this . . . again. It is also a political indictment. We know that these people were casualties of a war that would not have happened without the policies and guns and planes and soldiers and rhetoric and politics and global strategy of other countries beyond Cambodia's borders. The United States is near the top of that list of countries. We have a responsibility for the killing fields that was "Made in the U.S.A."

The skulls stacked up to the sky are there to make us accept our responsibility. And we do later as we sit with an eighteen-year-old artist who was orphaned by the Pol Potists and now draws for us what the killing looked like. His story is in outline like so many others': forced to leave his home, family members killed, lucky survival, the struggle of coming to terms with memory.

The Vietnam War Is Not Over

For most Americans Southeast Asia means the Vietnam War, and past history. It is history in the sense of a long-running bad experience that happened to us and then finally ended when the last Americans were helicoptered off the roof of the American embassy in Saigon in 1975. Of course, even to call what happened in Southeast Asia in the 1960s and 1970s the "Vietnam War" reflects our very narrow and self-centered approach to the world beyond our borders.

The Vietnam War was not just the conflict we think of in terms of U.S. soldiers and weapons used in an unsuccessful effort to keep the northern half of Vietnam led by Ho Chi Minh and his Communist regime from gaining control of the entire country. The Vietnam War was decades of conflict that did not begin with American attempts to prop up South Vietnam and did not end when American forces left Vietnam, a conflict that involved most of Southeast Asia and that continues even to this moment, a conflict in which American losses were small compared with the losses suffered by the "locals."

If the wall in Washington, D.C., that commemorates the U.S. war dead were extended to include all the Southeast Asians killed in the Indo-China war, it would stretch for many times its present length. This fact is not cited to diminish the worth of each American life lost, but to remind us of the necessity of reckoning the worth of each Asian death. What is more, except for the relatively small number of Americans still officially listed as "missing in action" or otherwise unaccounted for, the American memorial to the war dead is complete, a finished monument. If we were to include the Southeast Asian war dead, the wall would be an ongoing construction, with new names added each day to an ever-lengthening stone facade. And many of those names would be the names of children. These deaths come from "active fighting" in Cambodia and from the ongoing effects of battles fought long ago.

A recent report from Laos documents continuing destruction. Although Laos is mostly at peace—though economically devastated—children are still dying because of American weapons. In the 1970s the United States conducted unprecedented heavy bombing of Laos. Two and a half tons of bombs *per person* were dropped. But these words lie. "Were dropped" is a grammatical construction that works to hide who did the dropping. Americans dropped those bombs. American soldiers, even when they bombed secretly or as part of an open secret, acted as our agents, on our behalf.

We as Americans spread war and death and injury and destruction throughout Southeast Asia, and fifteen years later most Americans can't even remember the names of the countries involved or whom we favored and whom we opposed. Most Americans who grew to maturity after 1975 have no idea of what we did in Southeast Asia, and most who were of an age to know have already forgotten. A survey of American youth conducted in 1963, before the American stage of the Vietnam War heated up, revealed that almost no one could correctly identify North Vietnam's leader, Ho Chi Minh, but most could readily identify comedian Dick Van Dyke. More than twenty years later an informal replication of the survey revealed the same results: almost no one could identify Ho Chi Minh while almost everyone questioned knew who Dick Van Dyke was. Laos was then and is now a minor footnote for Americans.

The devastation in Laos due to American bombing was total in many areas, with no structures left in what once were thriving villages. The effects of that bombing are still not over. Children are *still* being killed or maimed by undetonated bombs that fell more than fifteen years ago but remain lethal, a triumph of technology over moral sense.

Throughout Indo-China children are in jeopardy today because of unexploded but still potentially deadly bombs and mines. We met a little boy on the street in Phnom Penh who was such a victim. He lost one leg in the countryside before his family moved to the city. Now he begs on the street as part of his family's attempt to survive devastating poverty. Despite the efforts of international humanitarian aid groups such as Handicap International that have been working at a feverish pace for years trying to catch up with the devastation wrought by the weapons, the country is so poor he has yet to receive a prosthesis.

In a Land of Victims

Laos and Vietnam suffered much from the war that ebbed and flowed in Southeast Asia from the 1940s until this very moment, but perhaps no nation has reaped the whirlwind as has Cambodia. During the period 1970–75, out of a population of less than nine million, in a country the size of Missouri, more than 10 percent of the population, nearly one million people, died in the civil war or as victims of American assaults on the warring parties (and "accidentally" in our attacks aimed at the Vietnamese who used Cambodia as a staging ground). To give some reference point for this we need only remember that during the American Civil War that "devastated" the South, "only" 2 percent of the Southern population died.

When the Cambodian civil war ended (for a time), and the Khmer Rouge emerged victorious, another million people died in Pol Pot's brutal program of national reorganization, a campaign that resembled genocide more than social change (some estimate the total deaths at closer to two million) (UNICEF 1990).

Then, in 1979, the Vietnamese intervened to put a stop to Pol Pot's Khmer Rouge, who were threatening Vietnam's border regions. Another 100,000 Cambodians were killed. The Vietnamese established a "sympathetic" government (what many called a "puppet" government) in Phnom Penh. According to Vietnamese military and civilian officials, they had "liberated" Cambodia from the Khmer Rouge.

But the Vietnamese "liberation" was an "occupation" from the point of view of many Cambodian nationalists. During the period from 1979 to the present more than 100,000 Cambodians have died in a "national resistance" war (UNICEF 1990). Killing goes on on both sides. Today, with the decline of Vietnam's allies in Europe (most notably the Soviet Union), the Phnom Penh government has become more militarily and economically vulnerable.

Fighting escalates as the nationalist resistance coalition sees a chance to gain ground after a decade of frustrating reversals. According to UNICEF estimates (UNICEF 1990), so many men have been killed in direct fighting and as the result of purges during the Khmer Rouge period that 64 percent of the adult population of Cambodia is female. This dramatic demographic imbalance has many implications for family relations and socialization.

Will peace ever come to Cambodia? Hopes rose in 1990, as a by-product of Big Power cooperation that seemed headed in the direction of forcing the resistance movement to make peace with the government in Phnom Penh under United Nations guidance. The proposed mechanism would be a Supreme National Council in which all factions—including the Khmer Rouge—would have representation. The Khmer Rouge?

It is often difficult for the uninitiated to believe, but the Khmer Rouge—and Pol Pot himself—have not disappeared. The Khmer Rouge were defeated by the Vietnamese and their Cambodian allies in 1979 (some of whom were themselves active in the Khmer Rouge but had lost out in internal power struggles or decided that the Pol Pot faction had gone too far or were too closely aligned with the Vietnamese to accept Pol Pot's anti-Vietnamese campaign). They retreated to the jungles and mountains of western Cambodia when the Vietnamese drove them from power. There they regrouped, sought support from the outside, and eventually received the support they needed from the Chinese.

Their Chinese allies have continued to support them. The Thais and the Americans have looked the other way (and have allowed support intended for other resistance groups to reach them). And they have found ways to generate independent income by signing commercial contracts for lumber and gem mining in the areas under their control. It is as if Adolf Hitler had not died in a bunker in Berlin in 1945, but had been permitted to withdraw to a villa in Austria to rebuild his Nazi movement and return to the political scene when conditions permitted. It is a nightmare come true.

When we visited Cambodia in 1990, there was much talk about "the return of the Khmer Rouge." Intelligence sources and popular rumor reported that the Khmer Rouge were on the move in the countryside again, winning military success, garnering peasant support (and sometimes coercing support when it was not readily forthcoming), portraying themselves as the leadership that can "once again free Cambodia from foreign domination" (only this time it is the domination not of the Americans or the French, but of the Khmer's traditional enemy, the Vietnamese).

During our visit we saw government soldiers on patrol in the countryside outside Phnom Penh. Rumors circulated about impending attacks on the city itself. A Khmer Rouge military commander in the field was quoted by a journalist as saying, "We are winning more easily than we expected. There is nothing that can stop us" (*Bangkok Post* 1990). Are Arn Chorn's worst nightmares about to become reality . . . again? How did it come to this?

History: It's Unlucky to Be Caught between Empires

Cambodia was once an imperial power in its own right. But in the fifteenth century the Siamese empire succeeded in conquering Cambodia and reducing it to a poor kingdom squeezed between Siam (Thailand) and Annam (Vietnam). In the mid-nineteenth century the French takeover of Southeast Asia led to the establishment of a protectorate in Cambodia. The political situation remained stable until World War II shook things up. The Japanese defeated the French and assumed colonial control. But Cambodia's fate continues to derive in large measure from the bad fortune of sitting between two powerful and competing forces, Thailand to the west and Vietnam to the east.

The post–World War II period saw an independent Cambodia under the leadership of Prince Sihanouk and relative detachment from the war in Vietnam and Laos until the mid-1960s. Then Cambodia became a staging area for North Vietnamese movement into South Vietnam, and it also became the site of a Communist insurgency of its own called the Khmer Rouge. The Khmer Rouge developed as an agrarian peasant revolt modeled on Chinese Communist lines and led by a group of radical intellectuals, most of whom (including Pol Pot) were educated in France. The early successes of the Khmer Rouge, coupled with the role of Cambodia in the Vietnam conflict, threatened American war interests. This threat eventually led to increasing American intervention in the form of massive bombing designed to blunt North Vietnamese movements and disrupt the activities of the Khmer Rouge. In 1970 American and South Vietnamese forces invaded eastern Cambodia, and Prince Sihanouk was overthrown by his prime minister, General Lon Nol.

You Can Change the World . . . But Unless You Know What You Are Doing, Please Don't

The goal of American policy was to continue a non-Communist Cambodia, to thwart the North Vietnamese and Viet Cong, to preserve

American influence and interests in the region, and to foster Western-style social and economic development. We sought to change the situation as it then existed in Cambodia. We succeeded, but with exactly the opposite results we had envisioned.

Between 1970 and 1973 American planes dropped 540,000 tons of bombs (250,000 in one six-month period), killing 150,000 people, mainly "civilians" in villages (Kiernan 1990). Ben Kiernan's report offers an example: "In 1971, the town of Angkor Borei in southwestern Cambodia was heavily bombed by American B-52s and Lon Nol's T-28s. It was burned and levelled. Whole families were trapped while hiding in trenches they had dug for protection underneath their homes. More than one hundred people were killed and two hundred houses destroyed, with only two or three houses left standing" (Kiernan 1990, 20).

Ironically, U.S. bombing contributed to the Khmer Rouge's success in taking over the country. Their military forces were effective, highly motivated, and adequately supported by China. Their political apparatus followed the American bombing, village by village, recruiting angry Cambodians to their cause of opposing the colonialists. The civil war intensified. In 1975 the Khmer Rouge won, and shortly thereafter the Pol Pot faction took control. American policymakers did not set out to destroy Cambodia, but they achieved that effect: they literally destroyed Cambodia in their efforts to "save" it.

Hell as a Matter of Political Policy: The Other Holocaust

The success of the Khmer Rouge and Pol Pot's dominance led to a program of genocide surpassed in this century only by the Turkish murder of Armenians and Nazi Germany's attempted extermination of the Jews and other "inferior" races. Not since Stalin's era had a government sought to destroy its own citizens on such a massive scale. A UNICEF report refers to this period as "some of the most dramatic events in recent world history" (UNICEF 1990, ix).

The Khmer Rouge forced the entire urban population into the countryside. All contact and commerce with the outside world was cut off. Currency was suspended. Education was terminated.

The capital city of Phnom Penh was forcibly evacuated, almost overnight. The Pol Potists considered the urban population to be corrupt and unforgivably Westernized. In 1974 the city's population stood at more than 2 million (having swelled from 500,000 in 1965 as a result of an influx of refugees from the war zones in the countryside). By 1978 the city's population had been reduced to a few thousand (mainly officials of the government, including those who ran special prisons and torture centers).

During this period, wearing eyeglasses was prima facie evidence of corruption and reason enough for a death sentence. Being a teacher was a capital crime. By 1979, almost all the children were unschooled (and even those who had been to school had largely lost whatever academic skills they may have had).

Massacres were common as the Khmer Rouge sought to destroy the entire infrastructure of the old regime and create a new peasant society. Some massacres were local events in which groups of rural Cambodians turned on people associated with Lon Nol's government. Others were systematic efforts of the Khmer Rouge to carry out its plan to purge Cambodia of foreign influences and create a classless peasant society. Still other massacres were the results of factional fights within the Khmer Rouge: the beast began to devour itself.

We visited one place where the destruction took place: Tuol Sleng prison in Phnom Penh. This former secondary school was turned into a site for torture and murder. Now it is a museum intended to document the genocidal policies of the Pol Pot regime. Here some 20,000 people died as the result of deprivation, torture, and execution. The Pol Pot regime kept good records of the carnage, including pictures and documents. Because the Khmer Rouge designated whole families as corrupt and traitorous, children were killed along with their parents. One wall of the prison is filled with the pictures of child victims. Another display links pictures of children with the pictures of their parents. It is hard to bear the walls of pictures.

The mechanisms of torture on display in the museum are carefully explained. Who would have thought to drown in this manner? What obscene ingenuity. The faces staring out at us from pictures on the wall are haunting. The very first person killed here was a fourteen-year-old boy whose only crime was being someone's son. We cannot forget that one of us has a fourteen-year-old son at home.

Many deaths during the Pol Pot time were the result of the harsh living and working conditions of the displaced populations. By 1978, the infant mortality rate had reached 263 per 1,000 births. Many children died of disease and malnutrition before they reached their eighth birthday, and a majority of the survivors were severely mal-nourished (UNICEF 1990). One of us has an eight-year-old at home.

There was no shortage of reasons to die in Cambodia in the late 1970s. According to a 1990 UNICEF report, "The enormity of the physical destruction, the psychological trauma, and the social dislo-cation were such that the first international observers to reach Cam-bodia in 1979 questioned the very survival of the Cambodian people" (UNICEF 1990, x). Estimates put the number of orphans at more than 250,000.

A Lost Generation

We think again of Arn Chorn as we sit in an orphanage—a "children's city"—after driving out from Phnom Penh into the countryside. Two young boys sit with us, one sixteen and the other seventeen. They have been produced in response to our request to have some kids draw pictures of Khmer life.

Both have the shy softness we have come to associate with Khmer youth. Both were orphaned as young children in the same disaster that befell Arn Chorn. One boy insists that he does not remember his early years, which is quite plausible given what we have been told about those experiences and what we know about the symp-toms of post traumatic stress disorder. And yet he draws vivid pic-tures of what happened. His artistic talent is impressive. Where do the scenes he draws come from? The explanation is simple. He has seen the pictures drawn and painted by others, and he has heard the same stories we have heard. He has been "indoctrinated" about the Pol Pot calamity as part of his teachers' and his government's pledge of "never again."

What are we to make of such indoctrination? We suspect that such "stories," such personal narratives, are an important resource in helping people cope with trauma and disaster. They give social meaning to personal experience. They provide a basis for interpret-ing the present and acting in the future. Such stories can be funda-mental to the process of coping with adversity.

Under Pol Pot, teenagers and children were recruited as enforcers and executioners. The film *The Killing Fields* documents what this bestial policy meant. The movie has become the public narrative through which Americans understand the Cambodian holocaust. But it is only part of the story.

While the Cambodian holocaust took place, the world stood by. As in the case of the destruction of European Jewry by the Nazi Third Reich, most of the world claimed ignorance. The United States—the country for which we are particularly responsible—allowed the killing fields to happen. What is worse, when the Vietnamese invaded and threw out Pol Pot's Khmer Rouge, we stood by and refused to help the surviving Cambodians. Despite 250,000 orphans and a shattered society we refused to get involved.

This is not to say that trying to help the Cambodians would have been easy. The Vietnamese were not a group of chivalrous knights in shining armor riding to the rescue of the Khmer people. In deposing the Khmer Rouge and consolidating their own control, Vietnamese forces displayed the kind of single-minded ruthlessness that permitted them to win their own thirty-year war of liberation.

For example, they were reluctant to permit private humanitarian groups to bring aid to refugees in western Cambodia who were caught in the fighting on the grounds that this aid would assist military resistance to their rule (Liv Ullmann, personal communication, 1990). They stopped a caravan of twenty trucks at the Thai-Cambodia border. What is more, they have been as brutal in suppressing dissent and nationalist opposition in Cambodia as they have been in Vietnam itself.

In 1982, after the emergency was over and the first years of "recovery" were past, per capita Cambodian income stood at $160. Cambodia was one of the poorest of the world's many poor nations, ranking 195th out of 203 countries whose per capita incomes could be calculated (UNICEF 1990). In 1987 the infant mortality rate was still above 100 per 1,000 and the death rate by age five was 206 per 1,000. One-third of Cambodia's children were chronically malnourished. Despite Cambodia's desperate need throughout these years, the United States refused to help. Why?

We refused to help because we had "lost" the Vietnam War, and because it was the Vietnamese who overthrew Pol Pot's Khmer Rouge. We refused to help because the government in Phnom Penh was a Communist- and a Vietnamese-dominated government. Instead of helping the Cambodians we funded the opposition, knowing that our actions meant more fighting. Never mind that hundreds of thousands of Cambodian children were in dire need. Never mind that we were unintentionally responsible for permitting the Khmer Rouge to take power in the first place. Never mind that funding the opposition guaranteed more dead and maimed children, and more orphans. We had to destroy those children to save them.

When the Allied blockade of Germany in World War I led to massive famine, humanitarian groups were formed to help the famine victims. In England the writer George Bernard Shaw was criticized as unpatriotic and traitorous for supporting these groups (one of which eventually became Save the Children). His reply was on the mark then and it remains pertinent today: "I have no enemies under seven years of age." Apparently we did have such enemies; the children of Cambodia were our enemies because they had the misfortune to live under the rule of a Vietnamese "puppet" government. This government is corrupt and has had a very poor human rights record, but that is not why we have opposed it.

The American refusal to help Cambodia because of the Vietnamese presence seems a rather childish response. We may be generous victors, but we do hold a grudge when we lose. Moreover, the United States government wanted to nurture its relationship with the Chinese government, which supported the Khmer Rouge because the Chinese too bore a grudge against the Vietnamese, who were clients of the Soviet Union. The "Pentagon Papers" documents included memos revealing that U.S. policymakers quantified the reasons for fighting in Vietnam as 70 percent to avoid a humiliating defeat for U.S. foreign policy; 20 percent to keep South Vietnam from Chinese conquest; and 10 percent to "permit the people of South Vietnam a better, freer way of life" (Sheehan 1988, 535).

A supports B because B opposes C who are enemies of A who fear D who want to encourage E to make things difficult for C who have a traditional hostility toward E. An ancient Arabic adage argues that "the enemy of my enemy is my friend," but national leaders and policymakers often carry this basic principle to ridiculous extremes. The words "friend" and "enemy" take on new meaning. But no matter how the policymakers categorize them, civil wars, border wars, invasions, and all the other kinds of warfare always produce dead children, dead parents, and a haunted generation of survivors.

One hears a great deal about depression among the Khmer— particularly but not exclusively in the border refugee camps. It is little wonder: depression is often related to loss, and the Cambodians have suffered too much loss. Children of depressed parents are often in jeopardy because their parents become emotionally and functionally incapable of caring for them.

We talked with the director of a mental health program addressing the needs of Khmer women in a border camp with 160,000 residents. She estimated that 50 percent of the women are "seriously depressed." Their experience of loss, coupled with the current situation, makes this estimate seem all too plausible.

When we visited the camp in October 1990, most of the refugees who had any realistic opportunity for resettlement in a third country had already left. The initial optimism concerning a rapid political settlement in Cambodia, which would have allowed the remaining refugees to return home, had been eroded by bickering among the factions, and there was much talk about escalating fighting in the coming weeks when the dry season began (the traditional time for offensive operations in Indo-China).

Indeed, as we left the region, a newspaper in Bangkok ran a story headlined "Cambodians Crowd Camps in Thailand." The story reported that "Cambodians driven by hunger and fear of renewed fighting are trudging into refugee camps over the border in Thailand as United Nations officials grapple with the task of repatriating the hundreds of thousands already there." Officials estimate that some 34,000 Cambodians fled their country to Thailand in the year preceding our visit. And the fighting, the starving, the fear, the uncertainty, and the sickness continue. Little wonder when we asked one resident his view of the situation he said simply, "I'm fed up."

Life in Purgatory

The refugee camps are pivotal to the continuing civil war. Each camp is "managed" by one of the three antigovernment factions. The situation is not coincidental. We were told how food aid and admission to the camps were made contingent upon joining the resistance. For starving and dislocated people, that made it an absolute "seller's market." The United States and other countries have accepted this arrangement. It is a convenient way to create and sustain a mechanism for translating opposition to Vietnam into military pressure against the Phnom Penh government. And it serves Thailand's own interest in countering the Vietnamese and keeping the Khmer refugees from integrating into Thai society. The Thai military keeps the camps on a short leash—with military bases nearby and strict rules about anything that smacks of permanence (e.g., restrictions on advanced education for Khmer in the camps). In 1979, the Thai military rounded up 40,000 Cambodian refugees and forced them back over the border into a mine field. Some 10,000 people died in this horrible scene (Mullen 1988).

Like the Palestinian refugee camps in the Middle East, the Khmer camps on the Thai border serve a political function in the conflict. Humanitarian concerns are often subordinated to partisan political goals. Thus, the international agencies must search and stretch their minds and hearts to find acceptable ways to accommodate "the other agenda." The camps close at night to the outside aid groups; all foreigners must leave by 5:00 and not return until the next morning. What is it like to live there?

Many refugees in the camps survived the Pol Pot era and have escaped across the border since 1979. Some are active partisans of the faction that controls the camp. Many are just hoping for a little peace and prosperity and are willing to settle for mere survival.

Many camps highlight the tenuous nature of the situation facing the displaced Khmer. There is always the prospect of shelling from across the border. There are mine fields outside the camps and throughout western Cambodia. It is routine for casualties to be brought into the hospital. Sometimes these casualties are children.

There is conflict and violence between and within families in the camps—which can become lethal with the ready availability of guns and grenades. You can purchase a grenade in the black market for a small price. Domestic violence is common—wife beating and child abuse.

Health conditions in the camps are a problem. The international humanitarian groups often contend with painful moral dilemmas. They are very conscious of the necessity of meeting the basic human needs of the refugees while at the same time not creating "economic" incentives to encourage more refugees to flee Cambodia. In 1990 the standard ration for new entrants to the camps was about eight pounds of rice per week—enough to survive but hardly a rich diet. What is more, United Nations staff were not issuing regular supplies—of mosquito nets, cooking pots, or oil, for example—

in an effort to reduce the incentive to leave Cambodia and enter the camps.

How does one walk this fine line between politics and ethics? What is the standard of health care applicable to the camps? Should it duplicate what the Khmer inside Cambodia experience, where the Ministry of Social Action and Welfare can only budget $.32 per month per orphan? Should it duplicate the health care available to poor rural Thais, people so desperate that they often sell attractive children to the brothels of Bangkok for $400? Or should the standard of medical care duplicate the standard common in modern affluent societies?

We visited the pediatrics ward of a camp hospital one afternoon. Most of the direct medical care is provided by Khmer "medics" who have spent several years in course work and on-the-job training. An American pediatrician supervises, consults, and monitors (in part to try to stem the flow of medical supplies from the hospital to the black market). "A lot of children die here," he tells us. Most of the deaths are not directly attributable to the military conflict. But the dead and dying children are indirect casualties of the war. Some of the youngest children are children suffering from failure to thrive, and many of the older children are suffering from malnutrition.

Family disruption, the depression, and the poverty stimulate a lack of appropriate supervision. In an environment with many hazards—water trucks that sometimes back over children, reservoirs in which children drown, hidden munitions that may become playthings for children once discovered—this lack of supervision means many injuries. Close living conditions promote disease transmission—an outbreak of measles was in progress as we visited.

This was the world of Arn Chorn and his generation, the world he lived in after he escaped from the hell of Cambodia under the Pol Pot regime. But he was fortunate. He was one of the thousands of Cambodian children and youth who have been to hell and escaped to "normal" lives outside Cambodia that seem like heaven in comparison.

A Sense of Mission

Many Khmer survivors have a sense of mission that is common among those who have come face to face with death and destruction and yet have managed to survive. They feel a moral obligation to live exemplary lives, to make a statement about the human spirit, a statement about what matters and what one can do in the world.

We asked the director of an orphanage in Phnom Penh about revenge. She herself had survived the Pol Pot era by escaping to the remote countryside to live among a small band of mountain people. A teacher since 1960, she was widely known in Phnom Penh and realized that to escape detection as a criminal (being an educated person was a capital crime), she would have to go where no one would know her fatal secret. Her husband, a sports star, was taken to a "reeducation camp." Her three children, the eldest of whom then was twelve, were separated from her and from each other. When liberation came in 1979, she found that the entire family had survived. But all had witnessed much horror.

Her experience as a teacher—and a survivor—prepared her to work in a newly opened orphanage. She decided to help children as a way of taking revenge against the Khmer Rouge. With her strong sense of mission, she represents the best of those who have remained in Cambodia despite the hard times and the political difficulties that have accompanied the Vietnamese-dominated era since 1979.

She told us that over the years the children at the orphanage have spoken often of revenge, but revenge not in the sense of killing, but of working to ensure that the Pol Potists can never return to power. The orphans are drawn to service in the new government, in the various ministries, or in the army. There are many reports of corruption in the process of recruiting soldiers for the Phnom Penh government (as there are for the various factions opposing it). And there is the problem of corruption—graft that draws some people to the government as an opportunity to misuse authority. But these orphans want to make a commitment to a new order. They want to rebuild the country, make it strong as a way to protect themselves and to honor those who perished.

Each year on 20 May, the government of Cambodia celebrates Commemoration Day, a special day of remembrance for all those who died under Pol Pot. It is an integrating ritual, similar in purpose and effect to the day set aside by the Israelis each year to remember the victims of the *Jewish* Holocaust.

For Zionist Jews, as for the Khmer of Phnom Penh, there is a political answer to their greatest fear: what if they come for us again?

This thinking underlies much of the current government's repressive approach to dissent and uncertainty (and it certainly is repressive, with reports of brutal prison conditions characteristic of authoritarian states). Seeing this in the Cambodian situation will prove helpful in understanding the Israeli occupation of the West Bank and Gaza Strip, and the dynamics of the Palestinian-Israeli conflict. A traumatized people carries with it a collective narrative that shapes political life and provides the foundation for the messages communicated to children of the next generation.

An interesting clinical footnote emerges in our discussions about Commemoration Day. When we ask a group of adult survivors of the Pol Pot era for the date of Commemoration Day, they falter and fumble with the task of remembering. One, an intelligent man in his late thirties who works as a language teacher and translator, says, "I have trouble remembering things." We ask how old he was when as a medical student he had to leave Phnom Penh. "I don't remember." How old was he when he had to sleep in the fields and eat leaves from the trees to survive? "I don't remember." How old was he when his sisters and brothers were killed? "I don't remember." Impaired memory is a common symptom of post traumatic stress disorder.

Making Sense of the Senseless

Most Khmer children have triumphed over the madness we might expect to find among those who have been subjected to the terror of the Cambodian holocaust. Their very success reinforces our principal hypothesis about the crucial importance of a child's basic relationships as the foundation for resilience and recovery.

Children who are "unaccompanied" are at greatest risk. They are doubly at risk not only because of the fact of their loss, but because of its nature, the process of losing. It is a devastation of primary importance to have lost one's parents. But to have "lost" them as so many in Cambodia have is too much to bear. Children who see their parents killed in front of their eyes—shot, beheaded, disemboweled, drowned, strangled—are most likely to manifest functional problems, the classic psychiatric problems related to trauma.

A child can reformulate a world without parents, *if* the other significant components of the child's life remain constant. A child can reformulate a world in which horror is a fact not a fantasy. But how can children manage to cope when all axes of reality are warping at once? It is as if they were faced with an impossible problem of psychic algebra: solve the equation $X = Y$ in which both X and Y are suddenly unknowns.

Robert Coles describes confronting such a child:

> As he talks and talks, I wonder that he is still alive and able to be coherent, never mind attend classes and get through week after week of this life. He saw both parents die before his eyes at age five. No wonder he is tired so often, and guarded, and fearful, and a "problem" to his good and sensitive teachers, who also have their "limits," and who accordingly expect that a psychiatrist might come up with some new ways of putting into words what happens when unspeakable political tragedies are visited upon those who have to suffer them on the ground—as opposed to those who plan them in the government buildings of countries far removed, including our own. (Coles 1982, 269)

For some children the loss comes quickly, dramatically: a shell explodes, a gun is fired, a grenade blows up. For others, the loss comes more slowly. At a border camp we met a twelve-year-old girl who exemplified the process of slow loss that is intrinsic to warfare of the modern sort. We met her at the camp hospital's "Feeding Center." To be eligible for supplemental feeding, a young child or infant must be less than the 25th percentile rank for weight. In other words, the child must be seriously malnourished to be eligible for the program. To participate, the child and a caregiver (mother, older sister, grandmother) come for most of the day, from 7:30 A.M. until 2:30 P.M. They receive milk, cereal, and vegetables to boost growth. When they reach the target weight (usually after several weeks or months of supplementary feeding) they must be dropped from the program.

Seeing children improve is encouraging for those who work there in the hospital, but seeing the same children return again a few months later after the basic insufficiency of their diet takes its toll again is frustrating and discouraging. But that is not the worst part. Staff must deal with hungry older siblings who show up in hopes of getting more food themselves. What does it do to a staff member who must refuse to feed a hungry seven-year-old because only his younger sister is malnourished enough to qualify for the program? This is the context in which we met the twelve-year-old victim of the slow war.

She carried in her arms her eleven-month-old brother, who was enrolled in the feeding program. Their father had been absent in the war for most of the last five years, and had been totally absent since the birth of the youngest child. Several months ago the mother also left, leaving the twelve-year-old girl in charge. The mother had finally succumbed to the corrosive effects of her isolation and deprivation. She had abandoned her children. There is nothing worse for a mother, and that she did it tells us something about the desperateness of her own situation; it was too much to bear.

Too much for an adult to bear? How can this little girl bear it? A neighbor has taken in the children, but the twelve-year-old is responsible for the care of her younger brother. That is why she is here at the Feeding Center with him. She hangs back a bit as we offer an impromptu puppet show (our favorite icebreaker with children everywhere). Looking at her sad smile and her flickering hopes, we wonder how we can bear this unbearable sadness all around us every moment here but made specific in the face of this individual child.

When people learn that we are traveling to war zones and refugee camps to "study" children, they often ask "How can you bear it?" On the plane from the United States to Thailand at the start of this trip, we sat next to a young woman on her way to a business meeting in Bangkok. She expected to be absent from home about a week and felt guilty about leaving her eight-month-old son behind for such a long time. She shed a few tears when we talked about this separation. When she learned where we were going and what we were doing, she said, "How can you bear it? I would be sobbing all the time to see what you are seeing." How do we bear it?

Sitting with the twelve-year-old abandoned "little" mother as she held her baby brother, bearing it was very hard indeed. We wanted to gather her up and take her with us, to give her a home, to try to fill the void in her life. But we couldn't, even if we really tried. She is a "displaced person" with no options. She must stay in the camp and eventually be returned ("repatriated") to Cambodia. In another time and place we might have found some way to reduce the number of abandoned Khmer children by one or two. But here we can't even do that.

And then we stiffen ourselves to the task of getting on with it. As our vehicle pulls away from the hospital compound she and her brother are still there waiting, still with a smile. We leave, but they must stay. How often have we heard that from the humanitarians who work in and with the camps. Talk to them about the difficult conditions under which they work and they reply, "Yes, but we get to leave and they have to stay." It may not say it all, but it says a great deal about the way things are. There are two classes of people in the world, those who get to leave and those who have to stay. Is there really much more to be said about the essential meaning of freedom?

Beyond Survival

Khmer on the border are still in crisis; their identities are uncertain. They have no clear path to the future. But the survivors in Phnom Penh are a different story. Yes, they face a constant daily struggle. Making a living is an omnipresent challenge; there are severe limits on the livelihood of many poor women. Phnom Penh's masses are very poor indeed. Only 50 percent even have access to a latrine. Walking the streets of Phnom Penh, we observe that most of the population seems to be "camping out" in the city rather than actually residing there.

One of the international aid workers in the city confirms this reality. Many of those now living in Phnom Penh have their immediate roots in the countryside. When people repopulated the city after the Pol Potists were deposed, they tended to become urban homesteaders. Only the week before we visited, a government sweep had succeeded in moving hundreds of families off the sidewalks and the grounds of public facilities (such as temples) where they had been living.

The people of Phnom Penh live in a politically ambiguous situation, even after the mild "reforms" of the last couple of years. Their government is, after all, no democracy. There is a controlling political force behind the seemingly unregulated activity that begins at dawn each day and continues unabated until dark. A 9 P.M. curfew is in force every night, and police abound. People who object may "disappear." The government suffers from corruption, some of which seems necessary for government employees to survive economically. A doctor's salary is equivalent to $6.00 per month; only by supplementing that meager income "on the side" can a physician make ends meet. One international aid official estimates that in some organizations 90 percent of all the material sent to the country is diverted to the black market (this is true in the border camps as well).

This is all true. And yet the survivors of Phnom Penh do have a place, a social and cultural position, an identity with a future, a homeland. In a sense that the refugee population cannot approximate, no matter how secure their camps or their new national surroundings, the survivors of Phnom Penh are *home*. They are rebuilding a nation, and they have among their many diverse interests a superordinate goal: never again the regime of the Pol Potists.

The survivors of Phnom Penh face many problems. There is the problem of memory and all the other sequelea of having lived through horrible trauma. There is the very real fear that the resistance will triumph and they will be caught in the middle or be punished for having been on the "wrong" side. But there is also the motivating challenge of rebuilding and re-creating and bearing witness.

The "tour guide" at the genocide museum told us of how, as a teenager, he was made a fisherman in the countryside. Because he could not swim he lived in constant dread of drowning. The river in which he fished and from which he had to draw drinking water often ran black with the decomposing corpses of other children and adults, victims taken away from the work camps for "meetings" from which they never returned. He has bad dreams sometimes. But we think that what has set him to healing is the work he does now, making a statement about the past and his survival. He wants to tell his story, and it has closure. He is here now bearing witness and doing his small part to ensure that "never again" will his fate be forfeit.

The director of an infant development and rehabilitation center presents an interesting and illuminating perspective on the process of healing. The center enrolls abandoned and orphaned young children. The children are six or younger, so none of these orphans is a direct product of the Pol Pot era. But the staff are.

The center hires teenage girls who were themselves orphaned as young children under the Pol Pot regime to serve as caregivers.

"They often need special training," the director tells us. Many of these teenagers do not know what it means to mother a child because they themselves have no experience or memory of being mothered. The director continues, "I tell them: Think of what you would have wanted from a mother when you were a child, and give it to this child now." It's a particular form of the "processing" of traumatic experiences that we believe is crucial to overcoming those experiences. It is clearly linked to the concept of positive revenge that so often comes up in discussions with Khmer victims.

Where have we heard this message before? Not "Do unto others as was done unto you," but "Do unto this child as you would have had done unto the child you once were." It's golden advice. Visiting with some of the young women and the infants they are caring for, we observed that they take this advice very seriously. These teenagers have been hurt. That is clear from their stories, and even in the way they seem hungry for connection and approval. But these young women are also individuals who are healing themselves through the active process of caring. That may be the key to the very future of Khmer society: healing through caring.

A Matter of Spirit

Why does one care? After having been through horror and having suffered great loss, why does a person continue to care? It is common to define an optimist as someone who sees four ounces of milk in an eight-ounce glass and judges it to be half-full, and a pessimist as someone who looks at the same glass and calls it half-empty. But this definition does not help us to understand the way people respond to profound trauma and loss such as has befallen the people of Cambodia. For such people, it is the capacity to look at a glass with only a few drops in it and believe in the possibility of refilling it someday that predicts successful coping. What resources do Khmer children have to meet this challenge?

It seems their Buddhist religion often provides concepts and rituals that prove helpful. After trying to suppress Buddhism for nearly a decade, the Vietnamese-dominated Phnom Penh government has reinstated it as the official state religion. The persistence of this religious impulse in the face of political suppression is a clue to its importance in the life of the Khmer people. The Buddhist emphasis on remembering and honoring the spirits of those now dead can provide a useful sense of connection that can help comfort an orphaned child. Many Khmer mention this. As we come to understand the process of coping with trauma this spiritual dimension takes on increasing importance as an explanation for why some succeed and others don't.

Beyond the spiritual as a matter of individual worldview, there is the spiritual basis for collective responsibility. The strength of extended family relations and the willingness of neighbors to take in abandoned or orphaned children are based in part on a spiritual commitment to the interconnection of lives. What is more, from a psychological perspective, it gives those children a model of caring that is very useful as fuel for the coping process.

Observers often mention the shy charm of the Khmer people. This seems readily apparent to the visitor, and may help to explain the intense commitments made by Western humanitarian professionals. They seem to like these people with a great deal of warmth and conviction (something that is not automatic in such situations, as our own observations of other refugee situations involving other cultures confirm). We felt this way, too. After only a short time in their midst we liked the Khmer. This makes the Pol Pot travesty seem even more nasty, distorted, warped, and perverse. One often wonders how these people could have produced those people.

The avowed aim of the Khmer Rouge was to rid the Khmer of "foreign corruption." Ironically, the means chosen—so draconian, bestial, and fanatic—seem so unlike Khmer culture as we understand it. It must be there somewhere, of course, and in struggling to find it we naturally think of Nazi Germany.

Many European commentators at first seemed perplexed that it was Germany, with its tradition of "high culture" and refinement, that produced the bestial horror of Nazism and the Jewish Holocaust. Others could see in the tradition of authoritarianism and anti-Semitism a ready cultural climate for what happened.

Is there a parallel in Khmer culture? We must leave that for anthropologists to figure out. But we suspect the answer to this puzzle is simpler and more disturbing. Most of us want to believe that "It can't happen here." We want to believe that only bad people do terrible things. We want to believe that evil has an easily recognizable face, and that its face is not our own.

Sometimes when people in Phnom Penh told us about "the Pol Potists" it sounded as if they were talking about some other race, not their cousins. After all, some of these people were with the Khmer Rouge until they repudiated the Pol Potists (for whatever reason). We have heard this same sort of distancing among Germans when they speak of the Nazis: they are not us. But we think the answer is much more social and historical than it is cultural.

Pol Pot's strength was greatest among the rural peasantry. Thinking about what they did, we were reminded of the slaughters associated with the revolution and civil war in the Soviet Union of the 1920s. There, too, ideologically driven madness arose from the combination of fanatic leaders (who found their psychological and intellectual needs met in an extreme revolutionary ideology) with rough peasants (who had bitter grievances coupled with a primitive sense of the place of violence in day-to-day life born of grinding deprivation).

And the reactionary forces could match the revolutionaries with their own brand of barbarism (which generally exceeded the level of viciousness characteristic of the revolutionaries). One need only read Mikhail Sholokhov's *And Quiet Flows the Don* and *The Don Flows Quietly to the Sea* to see what this combination can mean in terms of political depravity.

Perhaps every culture contains the bad seed that came to flower under the Pol Potists, just as every culture contains the counter-theme of compassion and life-cherishing morality, an ethic of caring rather than destruction. The British writer/philosopher C. S. Lewis certainly thought so. In his trilogy on good and evil which culminates in *That Hideous Strength,* he offered the hypothesis that each culture and society contains within it a distinctive character, a character that provides the foundation for its greatest good achievements and its most diabolical evil deeds.

Maybe it is the very primitiveness of the killing fields in Cambodia that disturbs us so much and prompts us to look for cultural explanations. How are we to understand people who have smashed the skulls of babies on trees and tossed the corpses into a ditch?

But there is no easy answer to be found in some simplistic and false concept such as "Asian disregard for human life." If it's killing and destruction we seek to explain, first let's understand how Americans could obliterate towns and villages and kill thousands with our impersonal bombing. Let's not forget that when faced with Vietnamese rebellion against their colonial rule in 1946, the French bombarded the city of Hanoi, killing thousands in the process (Karnow 1983). Let's recall the slaughter of millions of Jews under the Nazis, and the slaughter of peasants in the Soviet Union, the slaughter of Armenians by the Turks, of Kurds by the Iraqis, and let us not forget the slaughter of the native population of the American continents, North and South, by the "civilized" European invaders.

Perhaps the best we can expect from a culture is that it have resources to bring to bear in times of stress and trauma, resources that can help the healing process and stem the tide of situationally induced evil. The disintegration and violence observed among the Khmer in some of the border camps might be much worse in the absence of the virtues of traditional Khmer culture. As bad as it is, it could be worse. That is helpful to know, although little consolation to the increasing numbers of abused children and battered wives.

After the Emergency: Rebuilding a Nation

The period from 1979 to 1982 in Cambodia is called "The Emergency" by the international aid community. This small group of dedicated helpers had as its goal during the emergency period the very survival of the Khmer people. When they arrived in 1979, they found a people near starvation and in a state of utter exhaustion. Many had survived for an extended period on less than two hundred grams of rice per day. Everyone, including children, had been required to work eighteen hours of manual labor per day. One in four babies never reached its first birthday.

By 1982, this initial period of crisis gave way to reconstruction and redevelopment—even as war continued in the Thai-Cambodia border region. But international isolation persisted as part of the political power games in which Cambodia has been part of the equipment. The Vietnamese "powers that be" in Phnom Penh have certainly done their part to bend the work of reconstruction to fit their own political agenda. There is blame enough for all here.

Reconstructing all the institutions that provide the foundation for child welfare and health has proved an enormous task in this situation of extreme poverty, ongoing military conflict, and political machinations. But it has proceeded.

If we remember that only 50 physicians survived in the country, and that more than 15,000 of the country's 20,000 teachers either had died or left the country, the current situation is encouraging. Every analysis in Cambodia must start with such a statement of relative comparison.

When more than 5,000 primary schools reopened in 1979, they had no materials, few teachers, and faced a million eight- to fourteen-year-olds who had either never been to school or for whom schooling was only a vague and distant memory. Ten years later, there are 55,000 primary teachers who have received some training, and 90 percent of the children are enrolled in primary school—150,000 new six-year-olds per year (UNICEF 1990). The national standard is five years of general education followed by six years of secondary education.

In traditional Khmer society, orphans were cared for and integrated into kinship groups. Thus, in 1970, there were only three orphanages in all of Cambodia, serving 160 children. By 1974, as the disruption of the war increased, the number of children in orphanages had grown to more than 3,000. By the end of the Pol Pot era, the estimated number of orphans in need of care was on the order of 250,000. In response to the emergency, families adopted children, makeshift and transitional care centers were established, and various foster care arrangements were implemented. According to the Ministry of Social Action, by the end of the 1980s, most of Cambodia's orphans had been resettled with families.

We visited an orphanage in Phnom Penh whose history illustrates the orphan problem in Cambodia. In 1979 Vietnamese soldiers gathered together thousands of orphans as they swept away Pol Pot's force. Some 105 of these were brought together to form the nucleus of the orphanage. By 1981, there were 560 orphans at the facility, as more and more kids were found or simply showed up as the city of Phnom Penh was repopulated. In 1982 there were 473. By the time we visited in 1990, there were only 245 children.

The survivors of Phnom Penh are not without problems. No. They live with an authoritarian and repressive government. There is only a very slow development of political rights. There is the problem of the Vietnamese "powers that be." There are the problems of conscription and corruption. Some who live in the border camps have heard tales of oppression from those who have lived in Phnom

Penh and left to escape conditions there. Some in the camps are quite vehement on this point.

They see Phnom Penh as the heart of darkness, a puppet of the Vietnamese "oppressors," and the resistance as the good guys who will bring freedom and prosperity. Representatives of the Phnom Penh government describe themselves as the good guys who are all that stands between the Khmer people and a return to the ravages of the Pol Potists. We found ourselves with no easy task if we were to identify the real "good guys." If we had enemies, it was those who could and would justify more killing in the name of something else.

There are many realities in and around Cambodia. Sorting them out—let alone reconciling them—is not an easy task. We do not envy those whose job it will be to facilitate the repatriation of the refugees on the border and aid their reintegration into Cambodian society. We settled for understanding that the real issue here (as always and everywhere) is the fate of the children.

And the Future?

What will the future bring for the children of Cambodia? Even as we heard rumors of new military offensives, and heard the conflicting interpretations of reality to be found among the various factions fighting for control of the Khmer people, we hoped for peace. But even peace would have its dark side for Cambodia.

If the families currently located in the camps along the Thai border are allowed, encouraged, or forced to return "home," they will be exposed to the threats posed by more than a decade's accumulation of unexploded mines, booby traps, and other military explosives.

Thousands of accidental casualties caused by unexploded bombs, mines, etc., have already occurred in the border region. UNICEF expects many more casualties if repatriation takes place on a large scale and farm families seek to reoccupy rural communities that have been the scene of military activity. In the border region a new "Land Mine Awareness Program" has been started to deal with the problem of educating the Khmer people about this danger.

The International Red Cross believes that explosives will be more of a threat to returning children than malaria and inadequate sanitation in the affected areas. Here again, we have a grim reminder that the killing and maiming caused by modern warfare does not end when the shooting stops. Modern war is tenacious. It goes on and on and on.

One night in Phnom Penh we were catching up on some reading, a news magazine's special coverage of the United Nations World Summit on Children. It contained some cost comparisons that seem particularly relevant to what we saw in Cambodia. Worldwide, tens of thousands of children under the age of five die each day of diarrhea, measles, or malnutrition—more than fifty million children die over the course of a decade. What would it cost over a decade to save these lives by means of oral rehydration therapy, immunization, and food supplements? A group of experts has estimated the potential cost at about $2.5 billion, the *daily* cost of military expenditures for the world's governments. In the first weeks of the Persian Gulf war against Iraq, the United States was spending half a billion dollars a day, at a time when its schools and hospitals were starved for funds. As things stand now, this sort of calculation is merely a rhetorical exercise. How do we bear this fact?

4

Mozambique's Children:

Dying Is the Easy Part

"**W**hat is important in life?" a young child in Mozambique asked his grandfather. "Peace ... only peace," he responded (Supeta 1990). Like the children of Cambodia, the children of Mozambique are weary of war. But while the children of Cambodia are past the crisis, past the horror of the Pol Pot era, the children of Mozambique have not yet passed their crisis. Killing goes on. As we visited in early 1990, there was not even a rumor of peace. By the end of 1990, rumors of peace had begun to circulate in anticipation of multiparty elections promised by the government in the coming year. But there remains more death and destruction and dislocation and abandonment and deprivation. If Cambodia teaches us what war can mean for children when it becomes a holocaust, Mozambique can teach us what war can mean for children when it becomes a general condition of life.

War as the Black Man's Burden
and the White Man's Legacy

Mozambique sits on the southeast coast of Africa, where it is bordered by Tanzania, Malawi, Zambia, Zimbabwe, South Africa, and Swaziland. The east coast of Mozambique is a long and beautiful coastline that stretches for 1,544 miles on the Indian Ocean and attests to the great natural beauty of this country.

Mozambique was a Portuguese colony for several centuries, until independence was won in 1975. Portuguese remains the official language, but many local African dialects dominate the countryside. To convey the flavor of the Portuguese colonial period we need only report one incident, the Massacre at Mueda. One day in the spring of 1960 the colonial governor traveled to a provincial town for an official visit. He arrived to find an orderly delegation of several hundred Mozambicans who sought to present a petition of their grievances. This was done, and the crowd waited quietly and patiently for a response. The governor simply turned to his military commander and said, "Kill them." Government soldiers opened fire and shot several hundred people. This incident became a true "learning experience" for those who were fed up with colonial rule.

Leading the independence movement was the Front for the Liberation of Mozambique (FRELIMO), which was founded in the late 1960s and still continues in power. FRELIMO was led by Eduardo Mondlane, who became the first president after independence. FRELIMO's socialist programs appealed to the people's hope for their country's development and the improvement of their own life conditions.

Campaigns to open schools to all, to offer literacy programs, and to provide free health care attracted broad-based support, but the radical socialist ideology of FRELIMO and its open support for other black nationalist movements in southern Africa aroused the enmity of reactionary and white supremicist elements. Mozambique's official socialist ideology also angered the United States government, which imposed aid and trade restrictions that were only lifted in 1990.

Mozambique has been at war for most of its existence as an independent nation. The effects of the war have been devastating to the economic, social, and educational gains the government made following independence (*African Kora* 1990).

Bandits or Soldiers?

Although outsiders often refer to this conflict as a "civil war," most Mozambicans reject this term. They point out that a civil war is a war between geographical regions or political factions of the same nation. In Mozambique, the conflict is between the government and a terrorist force with little indigenous identity or support that is composed mainly of kidnapped men, women, and children, and relies upon outside, self-interested financial support to sustain itself.

The white supremacist Rhodesian government created, and the white supremacist South African government helped to support, the Mozambique National Resistance (MNR), more commonly known as Renamo. Its original purpose was to wage war against Mozambique's independence and deter it from supporting black nationalist movements in Rhodesia and South Africa. This purpose ended in fact with respect to Rhodesia when a black majority government came to power and the newly constituted country of Zimbabwe was formed. The purpose ended in principle with South Africa when Mozambique and South Africa signed a peace treaty called the Nkomati Accord in 1984. In recent years, as South Africa has moved toward an accommodation between its black majority and its white minority, official efforts by South Africa to destabilize Mozambique have diminished. But private sources within South Africa continue to support the efforts of Renamo. Today, Renamo is basically a loosely organized group of bandit gangs more interested in plunder than politics.

Since its formation in early 1970 by the Rhodesian colonial intelligence service, Renamo has been the instrument of an antigovernment revolt, violating Mozambique's borders and destroying the country's infrastructure. Fuel storage reserves, railroads, health facilities, and schools have been attacked, and thousands of civilians have been killed.

When Mozambique gave support to the struggle for independence by the black majority in Rhodesia, Renamo retaliated against the border villages. Renamo's brutal attacks have brought terror to the lives of Mozambican families, and that means children. A 1989 UNICEF report states that "out of the estimated 600,000 Mozambicans who have lost their lives as a direct or indirect consequence of the war, some 494,000 are children" (*African Kora* 1990).

The Renamo "banditos" have waged a war in the rural provinces of Mozambique that has caused more than 4.6 million people to flee their homes to find safety (UNICEF et al. 1990). Severe dislocation has left half of the population unable to feed itself and has had a profound effect on the country's overall self-sufficiency. Some Mozambicans have relocated to adjacent communities. Others have become refugees in neighboring countries. Still others have taken refuge in the capital city of Maputo, where the population has swelled to more than 1 million people—more than double its effective capacity. Additionally, the bandits have destroyed two-thirds of the country's schools and hundreds of health care facilities. Teachers, health care professionals, and relief workers have been tortured and murdered by Renamo.

Are There No Limits?

Kok Nam, a native Mozambican and photographer for the local *Tempo* newspaper, has covered a number of stories of Renamo atrocities. Commenting on some of the incidents, he expressed disbelief "that man could behave toward man as Renamo does." In Kok Nam's view, members of Renamo have no moral rules. He illustrated this conclusion with personal accounts of children forced by Renamo to witness the torture of their parents. "Renamo conscripts children into their bandit group and teaches them to take a knife and kill." He confesses that the brutality he has witnessed is impossible to understand.

He describes an incident that had occurred near the town of Ressano Garcia on the border of South Africa two days before we arrived in Mozambique. Renamo placed a bomb on the tracks to separate the engine of a passenger train from its cars. When the cars came to a halt, passengers began to jump from the train. As they jumped, Renamo fired at them, killing about seventy-five people. Three women survived the incident and were hospitalized. These survivors told how some of the other passengers were spared. Able-bodied men, women, and older children were ordered to carry valuable items from the train into the bush. Renamo instructed the young children to flee without their parents. Most of the children ran. However, as one mother's eyewitness account indicates, one three-year-old child refused to obey these orders. As he stood in his place, unwilling to leave his mother, a Renamo rebel machine-gunned him in full view of her and the other children. Few "armies" are so blatant and deliberate in making war on children as is Renamo.

Looking for a Moral Perspective

How do we find a moral or even a political meaning for this killing? The death toll for young children is staggering. It is estimated that war in southern Africa results in the death of twenty-five children every hour (UNICEF 1989, 10). Some children die in direct conflict with Renamo, and others die of hunger because the bandits burn their families' crops and steal or destroy their livestock.

The late president of Mozambique, Samora Machel, said that his country's children were "the flowers that never wither," but the war is turning the land that nourished these flowers to dust. In the period 1983–84 there was a famine in Mozambique. Some 100,000 people died because they did not have sufficient food. This famine was not the result of drought or flooding that destroyed crops. The war brought food production to a standstill. There were no products for export, and replanting the fields became impossible.

The bandits have made rural areas and farmland inaccessible by planting land mines. Emergency relief packages containing new seeds have no effective value because the seeds cannot be planted. The only safe mode of transportation to the provinces outside the capital is airplane, as we learned firsthand when we visited.

Malnutrition is the primary cause of death for children under the age of five. UNICEF estimates that half of the children living in Mozambique suffer from some form of malnutrition (UNICEF 1989, 16). The infant mortality rate in Mozambique is among the highest in the world, and only two-thirds of the children born survive their fifth birthday.

War Fought in the Stomachs of Children

Everywhere we went, workers with various nongovernmental and governmental organizations told us, "People are hungry." In fact, people are starving to death. One has only to walk the streets of Maputo for an afternoon to see thousands of undernourished children. Their thin arms and bulging stomachs and eyes are everpresent signs that the children of Mozambique are hungry.

There is not enough food to eat; shelter is overcrowded and in disrepair; and the water is not fit for drinking. In Mozambique only 13 percent of the people have access to clean water (UNICEF 1989, 15). Raw sewage runs on the sidewalk, and garbage is piled high on the street. Much of the housing stock is in the same deplorable physical state as public housing developments in Chicago. This reality is a telling commentary on both Mozambique and Chicago. It is not uncommon for as many as sixteen people to live in a two-room flat in Maputo.

The number of children in Maputo is overwhelming. They wear tattered clothing, no shoes, or shoes that obviously do not fit and are tied together with string or wire. Particularly striking was one girl of nine who carried a small baby on her back. She gazed for a long time into the window of a shoe shop, looking at all the brightly colored shoes of various styles. She herself had no shoes on her feet.

By Western standards Maputo is not a very safe place for children. Many children are injured daily, victims of unintentional injuries related to the crowded conditions, dense and unregulated vehicle traffic, and low level of adult supervision coupled with the unsanitary conditions and malnutrition. Compared with most of the country, however, Maputo is *the* safe place to live in Mozambique. The children play freely outside, inventing creative toys from found objects and taking part in an array of games that are often accompanied by rhythm and song.

Education

The first teachers' strike in modern Mozambique's history took place while we were in Mozambique. The strike began with peaceful demonstrations in a park near the Ministry of Education building in Maputo. The teachers danced and sang, and neighborhood children joined with them. Some of the teachers played volleyball to pass the time. But the peaceful demonstration soon became a battleground as police attacked the striking teachers.

On a Friday afternoon teachers gathered in front of the statue of former president Mondlane. The police fired tear gas on the crowd and dispersed teachers with clubs. One observer of the police violence described the stunned look on the faces of the crowd. Teachers are held in high esteem in Mozambique. Seeing them attacked by the police enraged the general public. Some observers confessed that their respect for the government plummeted.

The daily news reported that the government would not be able to meet the teachers' demands. The teachers originally presented the government with a list of fourteen demands, which they quickly reduced to seven. High on the list was a salary increase to two times their current pay of approximately twenty dollars per month.

The teachers work under very difficult circumstances. Books, paper, pens, and classroom furniture are in desperately short supply. Funds diverted to the military budget as a result of the war have seriously reduced resources for educational activities. Mozambican primary school enrollment stands at 46 percent. Only 3.5 percent of the population completes seventh grade. The current overall literacy rate is 38 percent, and for women it is 22 percent (UNICEF 1989, 16–17).

The Maputo schools are overcrowded. Much of the current situation is made all the more appalling because it is a consequence of the war: the steady progress toward development of the educational system following independence has been interrupted and undermined by the constant influx of people displaced by war and forced to take refuge in the city.

The Maputo schools have seventy children per classroom. The children are taught in three separate two and one-half hour shifts throughout the day beginning at 7:00 A.M. and ending at 2:30 P.M. Teachers are responsible for two shifts, but are only compensated for one and one-half shifts.

In Cambodia during the Pol Pot regime teachers were singled out as special targets. They supposedly represented "foreign corruption" and were marked for death. In Mozambique teachers are also special targets. But here their "sin" is that they are part of the "infrastructure" of the country. The goal of Renamo is to destroy that infrastructure in all its forms.

One relief worker with whom we talked observed that teachers have the same experiences with danger as the children. She said, "Teachers are trying to keep one step ahead of Renamo." Teachers have been attacked. Their schools have been destroyed. For example, in 1987 the province of Gaza had 120 schools, but today only three schools remain standing after Renamo attacks (UNICEF 1990). In Nampula province, Governor Jacob Nyambir reports that Renamo has forced 399 first-level primary schools (first to fifth grade) to close. This represents 35 percent of the school network in the province, and it affects the education of 36,000 children (UNICEF 1990). Since 1982 Renamo has destroyed 2,000 schools, thereby robbing 500,000 children of the opportunity for education.

Teachers have witnessed the capture of their students by Renamo, and they have seen students and their families murdered. Among the teachers' demands in the strike action was "combat pay" for assignment in the active war zones of Mozambique. Some of the teachers have lost everything they own, including their clothing and shoes, because of Renamo attacks.

One ninth-grade English-language teacher, Jorge Alberto, said, "The chalk gave me away." After the bandits burned his school down to the ground, they hunted for the teachers. Renamo found a box of chalk in Jorge's house, which betrayed his profession. He was fortunate: the local villagers helped him hide in the bush and then to escape (UNICEF 1990). But many teachers have not escaped Renamo terrorism. Teachers have lost their lives in the course of doing their job. In Nampula province, for example, seventy-five teachers have been killed (UNICEF 1990).

The armed conflict takes a heavy toll in the form of teachers' and children's lives. The psychological cost of the war is unmeasurable. UNICEF estimates that half a million children are at risk of psychological harm (1990). In one study, twenty-four of the thirty-five children interviewed had witnessed the violent deaths of people. Included in their stories were incidents of seeing people drowned, burned, buried alive, and shot (Reynolds 1989, 26). Children themselves are often tortured and injured by the bandits. A study of 110 Mozambican children aged seven to twelve who live in a refugee settlement camp in Zambia documents that 15 percent had been tortured or physically abused (McCallin 1989).

Street Children

It is difficult at first to identify street children in Maputo—most of the children are out on the street most of the time. Walking in the evening at 7:00 P.M., we saw three boys sleeping on the sidewalk. It was an extremely hot and steamy night. The children were dressed in tattered clothing and had no shoes. They were alone. We learned that these children were sleeping outside because it was cooler to sleep outdoors.

Another night we observed a group of eight children sleeping in a huddle on steps leading to an apartment flat. These children had no home. They slept entwined with their heads resting on each other's legs and arms. It was difficult to discriminate individual children in this silent mass.

Sitting outside one evening, we watched as another group of ten street boys looked for a place to sleep. Careful to find a shelter protected from the elements and safe from harm, they searched the stairways, hallways, and plant-covered walls of a cathedral. When they decided on a secure place, they laid down and formed the now familiar sleeping pattern.

In Maputo we visited a program for street children operated by a Catholic church. Located next door to the Loja Franca, a grocery store, the program enrolls children off the street. This is easily accomplished because many of the children stand outside the Loja to solicit money and goods. Thirty-two children between the ages of nine and eighteen were currently enrolled.

The program serves two categories of street children. Some children have been orphaned or abandoned and have no permanent home. Others have been separated from their parents because of the war. All of these children live at the center. Efforts are made to reunite the separated children with their families. The director proudly told us that she had been successful in nine out of twenty cases.

Some children live on the street because they have run away from home. Others were sent away from home by their family because they could no longer care for them. In Maputo, any program that offers shelter, food and water, and clothing to children is at risk of becoming a place where parents send children whom they can no longer support.

The director emphasized that the family in Mozambique is an extended family, extending even to unrelated people who are familiar with the child. Within this cultural framework, community members assume responsibility for the well-being of all the children. Mozambicans love their children, called "continuadoras," or those who carry life on. That there are so many unattached children in such a context is testimony to the extremity of the situation. For children to be abandoned in Mozambique means that the war has shredded the social fabric of community life.

The Front Lines Are Anywhere, Anytime

On the day we arrived at United Methodist Church's Inhambane Hospital, the hospital had one tank of diesel fuel in reserve. Thus, the ambulance would only be able to make one more run to transfer patients to and from the hospital. Reports indicated that there was no diesel fuel left in Maputo but that a shipment was in transit from South Africa.

The emergency plan was to send hospital staff out to the road to flag down drivers who might be willing to assist them in transporting the wounded and sick. To further complicate the situation, the hospital had run out of gauze, and clean water was in extremely short supply. Carolyn Belske, the hospital administrator, fights a constant battle for survival. Her priorities are the basics: blood, food, water, and electricity.

The hospital serves a district of 200,000 people. Included in the count are 1,200 orphans and 1,800 disabled individuals. There is one social worker for the entire district. There is only one psychiatrist in all of Mozambique. The hospital has one surgeon. He is the only surgeon in the province of Inhambane. There is one pediatrician and a nursing staff of two for the twenty-five-bed children's unit. Two physical therapists with aide-level training work with disabled patients.

Among the most common conditions treated at the hospital are anemia and parasitic disease. Almost everyone admitted to the hospital is suffering from malnutrition and malaria. Anemia is a complication of malaria. In the United States a hemoglobin count of 10 would be considered dangerously low; at Inhambane Hospital a count of 3 or 4 is common.

More than 90 percent of the children suffer from malnutrition. Malnourished children are more susceptible to other diseases. According to Carolyn Belske, they enter the hospital in "revolving-door style." About eight hundred children are admitted to the hospital each year.

Inhambane has natural barriers that tend to protect it from the fighting. On one side is the sea; on the other a crocodile-infested river. Nonetheless, Renamo attacks have occurred as close as two kilometers from the hospital. Even a strong military presence in the province has not prevented their attacks.

Inhambane Hospital staff have been faced with healing the physical and psychological traumas of the local population. These traumas often result from war crimes so heinous they seem unbelievable to anyone who thinks there are limits to what people will do to a man, woman, or child. Two years ago there was a massacre of three hundred people near the hospital. People were beheaded. Renamo took the heads to the village well and set them afloat in the water.

Staff have also directly experienced the terror of Renamo. The attending pastor of the hospital is one of their victims. Renamo burned his house and beat him, leaving him for dead. He now ministers to the spiritual needs of patients who have experienced similar traumatic events in their lives.

Hospital records are coded to track "guerra," or war-related, injuries. Separate accounts are kept for adults and children in this category. On the day we visited, the hospital admissions book included the names of fifteen children aged five through fourteen who had been injured because of the conflict. There were an equal number of abandoned children listed in the admissions book.

We made rounds with the attending physicians in both the adult and pediatric wards of the hospital. The hallways and rooms were crowded with patients and their family members. Parents kept vigil at the edge of their children's hospital beds. Mothers sat on the floor next to the beds, often nursing their babies. Many single beds were occupied by two children lying next to each other, feet to head. Though the staff is extremely committed, the conditions under which they work are constantly complicated by the lack of supplies and shortage of clean water.

The patients' wounds were left open because there was no gauze to cover them. When available, cloth rags were used for bandaging. The bedsheet stuck to the wounds of an eight-year-old who was suffering from third-degree burns caused by a Renamo attack on his family's hut. As the temperature rose, the smell of sickness and death pervaded the hospital rooms. Nothing is so disconcerting as observing the results of war at close range. The injuries caused to young and old alike by recent Renamo attacks confirmed the accounts we had received of their brutality toward civilians.

The surgeon put his arm under the shoulders of a nine-year-old boy who lay on his side in a hospital bed. As the doctor unwrapped the partially covered head of the child, he explained that the child's head had been "carved up" with a machete by a member of Renamo. A piece of the boy's cranium had been cut out, leaving a gaping hole that, as the surgeon explained, would never grow back together. In fact, the back of the boy's head would be extremely sensitive for the rest of his life, and he would not be able to sleep on his back because of the pressure it would cause.

In the next hospital bed was a boy of ten who had suffered a gunshot wound to his leg. The bullet missed the child's tibia but left a deep wound that exposed the bone. The doctor turned the boy toward us so we could see his injury. The child was in obvious pain. He did not look at us, and he was not able to focus on anything in the hospital room. There are no screens on the hospital windows, and insects buzz throughout the wards. With limited supplies of clean water and no gauze to cover the wounds, the likelihood of infection is high.

Two other recent admissions to the hospital were a father and his child. His wife, the mother of the child, had been killed in a recent bandit attack on their village. During the attack the child's hands and feet were burned by the bandits. The father, after witnessing his wife's murder and the torture of his son, managed to escape into the bush with the child. Soldiers later found them wandering in the countryside and brought them to the hospital in Inhambane. The child was recovering from his physical burn injuries, but both father and child will struggle with the psychological effects of their experience for a long time.

Smiling Is the Starting Point for Childhood Reclaimed

The pediatric ward was filled with infants, toddlers, and preschool children who suffered from extreme malnutrition. Some of the children were diagnosed with marasmus, a deficiency disease that results from lack of protein and inadequate calorie intake.

Mothers sat on the cement floor of the children's rooms, holding them and comforting them. The children were very sick. Their stomachs protruded, and the skin on their arms was wrinkled and thin. Children's legs were swollen with edema. They showed such signs of kwashiorkor as hair depigmentation and hair loss.

We found it difficult to discern the age of the children by observing them. Their growth had been stunted by lack of proper nourishment. One seven-month-old baby weighed only five kilos (twelve pounds). In the United States, the average weight for a one-month-old boy is eleven pounds and at six months, nineteen pounds (Iowa Curves, Jackson and Kelly 1945).

We observed the faces of children with little expression even when the staff attempted to elicit a response. Dr. Marion Jones, the attending physician, uses the children's desire to interact as a barometer for their improved health. She said that she can tell when children begin to feel better "because they start to smile."

There are degrees of malnutrition. Dr. Jones explained that some malnourished children can immediately begin to eat small amounts of food. The amount is increased gradually over time. These children can recover from the disease. In severe cases, however, the children's digestive system has ceased functioning and will no longer accept food. The food they eat is eliminated in the same form it was ingested. Severe cases are too common at Inhambane Hospital. In the week before we visited, five of six new children admitted had died.

Children who survive episodes of malnutrition are at risk for abnormal physical development. Research indicates that their central nervous system may suffer irreparable damage. During infancy the human brain gains weight at the rate of 1 to 2 milligrams per minute (1.5 grams per day). Malnourishment stunts this growth (Cravioto 1966). Furthermore, studies show that behavior and mental development are also affected. We observed that the hospitalized children were apathetic and showed little sign of the curiosity or desire to explore the environment that characterizes physically and emotionally robust children. Few smiles here.

Can You Remember *and* Survive?

Sometimes it is too much to remember. We learned that lesson in Cambodia. Remembering is too strong a challenge to any concept of a just world you still treasure after all you have seen and heard. We want to forget the sixty-year-old man we met at Inhambane Hospital. We want to, but know we will not succeed.

He was a victim of a Renamo invasion of his small village. When the surgeon brought us into his room, we noted the blank stare in his eyes. His eyes were glazed, and he made no eye contact with us. We were not sure whether he was in great pain or was psychologically disconnected from the environment. Renamo had cut off his penis with a machete. How does one go about psychologically recovering from such an assault? How do we recover from even knowing about it? How do professional helpers recover from living with such barbarity day in and day out?

The psychological effect of the war on hospital staff is evident. When 80 percent of the new child admissions in one week die from war-induced causes, staff openly question their ability to remain strong. Dr. Jones wondered whether she could go on because "it's so difficult emotionally."

In her role as hospital administrator, Carolyn Belske is aware that staff need emotional support. She observes that they cope by becoming psychologically numb. She said, "Staff suffer, but they show little emotion. But if it's encouraged, I wonder how they will survive." If feeling what you know is too much for adults, what about the children?

Childhood Abandoned

The war has left an estimated 200,000 orphaned and unaccompanied children in Mozambique (Boothby 1990). A national family tracing project sponsored by Save the Children (United States and United Kingdom) has successfully reunited 4,000 children. But many children remain in institutional care. We made two visits to the Infantario Provincial in Maxixe, Inhambane. This orphanage serves 60 children ranging from infants through children aged fifteen. Most of the children are war orphans. When we arrived the children were standing in the courtyard of the orphanage or sitting on the concrete floor in front of the building. Many of the children stared blankly at us, and we immediately observed the absence of toys or activities for the children.

Their clothes were tattered, and they themselves were very thin. Some of the children had open sores on their legs and arms. The director told us that the center did not have enough clean water, food, or clothes for the children. Their educational supplies were few, and daily program operation was extremely difficult. Under the circumstances, the center staff was functioning as well as they could. The facilities included large sleeping rooms for the children and a separate space for meals. There was a kitchen and laundry room.

The children in this center are orphaned because their parents were killed by Renamo, or they were separated from their parents when their villages were attacked by the bandits. Identifying the home village for very young children is often impossible; reunification in such cases can be a long and arduous process.

On the day we visited, a new group of school-age children had just been brought to the orphanage by the Mozambique military. These children had been kidnapped from their villages by Renamo and rescued from a bandit camp by the army. We interviewed this group of children to learn about their experience with Renamo.

One of the boys had spent three weeks with the bandits. He had been tending the family's cattle with his brother when the bandits came. His brother escaped, but the bandits took him away to their camp. He said, "The bandits are bad, they kill, and they beat people." When we asked him what should be done to the bandits, he said, "They should be killed."

Another boy was alone in his home, while his mother and brothers and sisters were away in the field working. They escaped, but he was captured by the bandits. He told us that while with the bandits, he had "no opportunity to be free." He said that he was "beaten for anything." He was forced by the bandits to steal food from nearby villages and bring it to them, but he himself was given very little food to eat. He said that the bandits questioned him, asking for the names of the men in his village who worked in the South African mines: "The men have money, and the bandits wanted to steal it." If he did not comply with their requests, they beat him.

One young girl spent three years with the bandits and said that her life in the bandit camp was very hard. There were other children in the camp, but they were not allowed to talk to each other. They were constantly under the watch of the bandits. While she was living in the camp she became ill. The bandits took the child to a witch doctor. The witch doctor told the bandits that she was sick because her grandfather had died and her mother needed her at home. He prescribed a cure: he gave her a live chicken to bring to the grave site and a jug of wine, which he instructed her to pour on her grandfather's grave. Then the bandits took the child back to their camp.

During the visit to the witch doctor, soldiers had invaded the camp. The bandits were captured, and the children released. The soldiers brought the girl to the orphanage. We observed, under a tree at the orphanage, the bottle of red wine wrapped in a traditional sarong cloth. The wine was beginning to leak through the cloth. A live chicken walked nearby. We were told that this was the chicken given to the girl by the witch doctor. She believes her grandfather has died in her absence, and she told us, "If I ever find my mother again, I will go to my grandfather's grave and do what the witch doctor said."

The lives of all these children have been disrupted by the bandits. Kidnapping and torturing children, and severing their family ties, have caused psychological wounds that are difficult to measure but easy to detect.

When Children Draw Pictures of Total War

Many of the children we interviewed were often quiet and sullen, particularly if they were separated from family. Frequently these children stared beyond us as we talked. What were they looking for? They displayed no joy or laughter in the time we spent with them. As we have done in other war zones, we asked some of these children to draw pictures for us. One boy drew a house and said, "No one lives in the house." Another child drew a picture of people walking and said, "They don't know where they are going." Yet another child drew a picture of an upside-down person. These pictures illustrate the empty, displaced, and confused world of these child victims of Renamo.

There are no boundaries between the war zone and the most private domains of their experience. For them life is total war. The combination of horrible experiences coupled with disrupted attachment relationships has set them adrift in a way that is frightening— to them and to the people who are supposed to care for them.

Who Will Fill the Empty World of an Orphan?

Of the 110 children served in both day and residential programs at the Xai Xai Orphanage, 40 were orphans living in permanent residence. They ranged in age from nine months to fourteen years. The children's records indicated that their parents were killed in the war or that they were separated from their parents during village attacks by Renamo. Twenty-three of the children had been kidnapped or forcibly dispersed from their homes by the bandits. Many of these children had wandered the rural countryside alone. They were found by the military and brought to the center.

The orphanage consists of a number of small houses, where children sleep and attend school. There is a large dining room and kitchen for food preparation. On the day we visited, activities were taking place outside. The older children and staff carried tables and chairs from the classroom and placed them in the shade of the trees. The facilities were comfortable, and the center had educational supplies for the children.

The staff worked with the children in such activities as drawing, singing, and dancing. After the children drew pictures, they stood individually to tell a story about their picture. One young boy made a particularly strong impression on us. He had fallen on a land mine while out playing and had lost both his legs at the knee. He was playing on a bridge that collapsed. Government soldiers had mined the area under the bridge as a deterrent to Renamo attacks. Thus his injuries were "accidental." After the incident, his parents separated because neither parent wanted the responsibility of caring for this child. So he was brought to the orphanage. He had no prostheses and no wheelchair. He scooted around on the sandy ground using his arms. He smiled often and participated in all the center activities with the other children. Somehow he has begun to fill in the gaping holes in his life.

When the children formed a circle to play a tag game, he joined them, and he took part in an organized relay race. His school friends encouraged him and allotted extra time for him to get to the finish line. It was clear that staff gave him a great deal of support. When we asked him to draw a picture for us, he drew a picture of the man who helped after he had been injured.

The loss of limbs, parents, and home has tested the limits of this child's resources as it would test any child—or adult for that matter. And yet he can still smile and laugh with his friends. We judged him to be what developmental psychologists would call a "resilient child." However, the strength he demonstrates against major adversity and the gains made in resiliency in war cannot compare with opportunities for development he would have had whole, in peace. Psychologist Norman Garmezy reminds us that "there are . . . few instances of coming through the fire storm without being harmed; growth that comes from adversity is a very dangerous concept" (Garmezy 1990). This boy's life is changed forever, and he faces major barriers to rehabilitation.

In Mozambique, the prospects for artificial limbs, physical therapy, and access to housing, education, and employment are extremely limited. The Red Cross has a program in Maputo Hospital to construct prostheses from local materials. The products are not sophisticated, and the demand far exceeds the resources. The villages have no pavement. The ground is dirt and sand. Wheelchair use is virtually impossible.

Families in Inhambane

We visited with families who live in the rural villages that surround the provincial capital city of Maxixe in Inhambane province. Nestled in the trees, the villages are composed of huts with thatch roofs. Huts are often grouped to accommodate extended family members. The result is a series of small neighborhood arrangements. Though many of the people who live in the village have been displaced by bandit attacks in their home villages, the sense of community among the family members with whom we visited was strong.

We observed people working cooperatively to grind corn manually, carry containers of water, and care for children. Many nongovernmental support services are provided to the villages by the Christian Council of Mozambique and the Lutheran Social Services of Inhambane. People in Maxixe do not have enough food or access to clean water. There is a false sense of safety in the village. Compared with Maputo, the villages of Maxixe are very quiet. However, it is much more dangerous.

One of the villages we visited was Rumbana, named for the former chief of the people. Many of the families who live in Rumbana have been displaced by the war. Some had been attacked by bandits and forced to leave their homes. Others were captured by Renamo and later managed to escape. Rumbana was perceived by the families as a safer place because of its distance from bandit activity. However, in recent months, attacks have occurred only two kilometers away.

Mothers expressed their heightened sense of danger in the interviews. One mother began by saying, "I have suffered a lot." She was living with her husband, three children, and her grandchildren in a nearby village. Her husband became very sick and died. She was left with very few resources and too many family responsibilities. She said that she was often without food for herself and the children. Survival was an issue they faced daily, in a way that few of us can truly understand.

The safety of her family was shattered when bandits attacked her village. The bandits searched all the homes for food and valuables. Since they had surrounded the village, there was no possibility of escape. The entire family was kidnapped. Two daughters were taken to one camp, and she, her third daughter, and her two grandchildren, aged one and two, were taken to another camp. The children had been separated from their mothers during this process.

Though she lived with the bandits, she never saw them; they sent other prisoners to give her orders. She reported that the bandits sexually abused young girls. Older women were forced to search for food for the bandits. She said that some of the older children were used as bandits. She further observed that women and children were drafted equally to fill the needs of the bandits.

Many people died in the camp, but she never gave up hope of regaining freedom. She and the other women in the camp often planned escape strategies. They were always watching for an opportunity to employ these plans. One day she was faced with the decision "to escape or to die." There was word that the army would soon attack the bandit camp. She said, "As soon as I had a chance, I ran like a gazelle into the bush with my daughter and the grandchildren." There she hid until the army captured the bandits.

This woman eventually found her brother-in-law, who helped her relocate in Rumbana. She does not know where her other two daughters are. She desperately wants to see them. She said, "I don't know if they are alive or dead." She also worries that her grandchildren will not recognize their mothers if they do return. When we asked her if she feels safe now, she replied, "I don't know if I could run enough to escape."

A Leg That Will Not Heal

We visited with a second family who had been displaced several times by the war. They had moved from their original village to Massinga, from there to Macuacua, and finally to Maxixe. The mother lives with her three sons and three daughters.

One of the daughters is mentally retarded. During an attack the bandits broke this young girl's leg in what was apparently an act of gratuitous brutality. They also destroyed the village hospital, leaving the families without accessible medical care. As a result, the child's leg healed in a fixed position. She cannot bend her leg. There is a deep scar on her thigh where the bandits hit her with a machete.

After the family settled for the third time, medical staff at Inhambane Hospital attempted to correct the problem, unsuccessfully. The child will never regain the use of her leg. We asked her to draw a picture of where she lives. She sat with the leg straight out in front of her, bending deeply to reach the paper and pens we had placed near her.

Her drawing consisted of extremely small human figures, drawn in one corner of the paper. What does it mean? Did she represent her physical limitations by her inability or unwillingness to use the whole space? Was she representing what she had seen, the powerlessness of people and their inability to protect themselves?

In 1985 the family was again forced to move. The mother reported that one morning the bandits came to the village and took many of the families' possessions. Later that same day the bandits returned and took more items. The mother recalled overhearing the bandits say, "It looks like they have much, and we will keep coming and coming until it is all gone." She prepared to escape from the village. When the bandits returned for the third time the next day, she waited until they were occupied with stealing from her neighbor, and then she fled to the bush. Figuring that the roads were not safe, she hid in the bush for two days.

When we asked this woman whether she now feels safe in her home, she responded, "I feel more safe, but I am starving." How the war and displacement undermines survival was poignantly presented in a story written by the oldest daughter in this family. She wrote, "In Mozambique, we live in a very disorganized way due to the enemy situation. We eat, but we do not eat all the crops. Thus, at my home, I am very much in need of food. Whenever the sun rose, I moved from place to place due to the enemy. And here I am: I have no job, I do nothing, so where can I get the food?"

What More Can Happen?

Physical conditions for children are so appalling in Mozambique that it is easy to lose sight of the quality of their internal experience, their subjective lives. This is understandable. To see children with their heads split open from machete attacks and children who have lost legs and sight to mine explosions screams out for some direct aid and comfort. And the psychological cost seems self-evident in many respects. The horror of witnessing your parents beheaded before your eyes must be traumatizing.

Indeed, to the extent that we can get beyond the physical conditions of life, the malnutrition, the disease, the poverty, the maiming wounds, we can and do see the spiritual challenge and the psychological neediness. Looking over our field notes we do find references to the need for psychological healing.

Some of the psychological need is simple and gross: the need for reunification with family and the need simply to feel safe. Some of the psychological need is more sophisticated: the need to clarify what life is all about and who you are as a person, now and in the future, when you have seen such terrible things and been forced to perpetrate such things yourself, and all before you turn thirteen. Children and childhood in Mozambique are under siege.

A study by the International Catholic Child Bureau in Geneva (McCallin 1989) analyzed data from interviews with 110 mothers and their children between the ages of seven and twelve. These interviews had focused on their experiences with Renamo violence in Mozambique. All of the families had left Mozambique because of bandit activities and were living in a refugee settlement camp in Zambia. Some 44 percent of the women and 20 percent of the children had witnessed a murder. Forty-five percent of the women and 19 percent of the children knew someone who had been injured by political violence. Thirty-two percent of the women and 15 percent of the children had been tortured.

In the same study, a group of 119 adolescent refugees from the same camp were interviewed. Forty-two percent had witnessed a murder, 44 percent knew someone who had been injured, and 18 percent had been tortured.

Men wage war. Children and their mothers suffer. War infringes on the basic human rights of children. They lose things that cannot be replaced: relationships with significant people, time, their childhood.

Life in Mozambique is hard to bear. And yet children and parents survive, and some even dare to hope. Those who hope have faith. Belief in life and the meaning of one's communal purpose is one of the basic necessities of life in a war zone if children and childhood are to have a chance. We discovered this truth in Cambodia, and we see it again here in Mozambique.

Their Hope Shames Us

"A Luta Continua!" (The struggle continues!) is a Mozambican phrase that we quickly learned upon our arrival. We heard it many times during our time in Mozambique, and we came to understand the complexity of its meaning for children and families.

Children play, sometimes in ways that are a delight for the observer, who is bombarded and numbed by the terrible things he or she learns about in Mozambique. One of the most inventive toys in evidence among the children of Mozambique was the "carlinio" (little car), a toy made out of silver wire with soda-can wheels. Simple designs looked like a small rectangular-shaped wagon with a long handle. The carlinio is pushed in front of the child. More elaborate designs included pickup trucks and double-decker buses that had windows, doors, and multiple wheel systems. The long handle often had a steering wheel at the top. The carlinio is constructed to have a carrying space. The children load cans and other found objects into the carlinio, and use it to transport small grocery items.

Children roll automobile tires down the street. They place a can inside the tire and place two sticks in it protruding from either side. The sticks are handles with which to roll the tire in front of the child. Groups of children have races with their tin toys. For a moment, at least, there is childhood in Mozambique. But tomorrow? And the next day?

Try to Remember

We visited Mozambique in early 1990. At that time the Renamo war was "old news" in the United States. Only rarely did it ever become a story in the national news media. Six months later it was still for the most part a nonstory. Today it is probably still absent from American national consciousness. Why?

It appears that one of two conditions must be met before a foreign war can become newsworthy in America. One is some special character of the assault: more people killed than in previous assaults, or people killed in new ways, or people killed in new places, or some new group of people killed. The second is the direct involvement of Americans: Americans killed, American interests threatened, American celebrities involved. The war in Mozambique is generally a nonstory for Americans because it does not meet either of these conditions. Incredible as it may sound, from the point of view of American newsworthiness, nothing ever happens in Mozambique.

When we traveled to Cambodia, the war was mainly in the past and the future. Yes, we were confronted with the long-term consequences of the war in psychological, economic, and social deprivation. But most of the grittiness of the war—the maiming and killing—was interpreted for us by the victims. For most of the Khmer we saw and with whom we spoke, the war was something from the past: the civil war that preceded the Khmer Rouge's rise to power in the early 1970s, the terrible years of Pol Pot from 1975 to 1979, the war of resistance to the Vietnamese from 1979 to the present.

To be sure, for some war was a current event. Although the battlefields were largely quiet when we visited at the end of the rainy season, "fresh casualties" were produced regularly. And increased fighting was anticipated in the weeks that would follow our visit, once the dry season began in earnest.

This was growing up in a "war zone," but in a way that was intellectualized in many ways. In contrast, Mozambique showed us growing up in a war zone with much greater immediacy. It required no imagination, no conceptualization. It was children with shattered bodies. It was dead bodies. It was bloody. It stank of injury and death.

"Once you've seen one massacre, you've seen them all," one observer noted, with callous precision. But once you have seen what a massacre means, you can never forget. We wish we could sometimes. We really do.

5

Nicaragua in Conflict:

The Politics of Suffering

What do you want to be when you grow up?

I don't know. . . . It doesn't matter. . . . I'll probably be killed like my father before then.

—Javier, age 10, April 1990

Javier is one of more than 15,000 Nicaraguan children whose mother, father, or both have been killed since the armed conflict between the Sandinistas and the Contras (a contraction of the Spanish word for counterrevolutionaries) began more than a decade ago. He is another orphan "Made in the U.S.A.," for those who killed his father acted under the direct sponsorship of the United States government. To the extent that any citizen is directly responsible for the actions of his or her government, we are responsible for Javier's loss. Our bullet killed his father. We sent it to the Contras in the name of some "higher purpose." Meeting other Javiers in Nicaragua, we thought again: "What higher purpose could there be than preserving and enhancing the life of a child?"

It is not a new question, of course. In Dostoyevsky's *Brothers Karamazov* a "story within the story" concerns Jesus Christ, who returns to life only to be interrogated by the Grand Inquisitor. The Inquisitor tells Christ that he is an unforgivable troublemaker, someone whom no one really wants to hear. At a critical point in making his case, the Inquisitor poses a special dilemma: would you be willing to torture a child to death if by so doing you could save the world?

Political leaders constantly answer this question with a "Yes," but they hide their decisions to kill children by referring to "policy goals" and "strategic interests." Somehow politicians always seem to conclude that the next child's death will be justifiable because it will be the one that really will save the world. For what? For democracy? For peace? For oil? For capitalism? For our national interest?

Nicaragua is a country about the size of Iowa, with a population roughly equivalent to that of Chicago. Approximately 500,000 of the nation's 1.8 million children under age seventeen have been directly affected by the armed conflict; they have suffered the disruption of their education, the destruction of their schools, displacement from their homes, physical injuries, kidnapping, and the murder of their parents, siblings, and other relatives. Five hundred thousand children.

If we were to translate those numbers to the United States, that would work out to more than twenty million children. This kind of disruption would be unthinkable. That's part of what civil war is, of course, unthinkable. During the American Civil War 130 years ago, 2 percent of the entire population was killed. Few people escaped some impact. And what if Great Britain or some major European power had actively supported the Southern cause with supplies and weapons and sponsorship? The deaths would have reached greater proportions, the suffering increased. Slavery would have continued its cancerous hold on the American soul for still longer.

We Americans have a special responsibility for the people of Nicaragua, especially the children. For more than a century the fate of Nicaragua and its people has been tied to decisions made in the United States. Like much of Central America, Nicaragua has had to contend with the practical ramifications of America's belief in its Manifest Destiny and its promulgation of the Monroe Doctrine. The former asserted that the entire North American continent was intended by God for the United States. The latter asserted that the Caribbean, Latin America, and South America fell within the United States' sphere of influence and that the United States had a right to prevent foreign intervention in these areas and to supervise their political and economic developments.

In Latin America, these two American beliefs always have a strong influence on local political and economic events and often become the dominant force in day-to-day life. Americans have intervened directly in Nicaragua many times since the mid-nineteenth century. At one extreme was the individual adventurism of William Walker of Tennessee, who with a band of followers and mercenaries invaded Nicaragua in 1855 and sought to establish himself as its dictator. With the slogan "five or none" he tried unsuccessfully to seize the other four Central American countries and unify Central America into a republic supporting slavery, hoping thereby to strengthen the South's case against abolitionists in the North.

At the more conventional end of the spectrum, U.S. military forces have been used repeatedly to force Nicaragua to heed American demands. In 1927, for example, U.S. Marines invaded Nicaragua to put a stop to a populist insurrection led by the charismatic leader Cesar Augusto Sandino. In 1926 Sandino had taken up arms in support of Vice President Juan Bautista Saucasa, who had staked a claim to the presidency on a platform that challenged the dominance of the United States and its political allies within Nicaragua. Sandino's success led to growing frustration on the part of the United States government. Partially in response to anti-American feeling mobilized by Sandino in Nicaragua, President Franklin Roosevelt announced a shift in U.S. policy regarding all its southern neighbors. Henceforth, the United States would follow a "Good Neighbor Policy."

In 1933 Saucasa was inaugurated president of Nicaragua, and American marines withdrew, although the influence of the United States on the local scene remained strong. On 23 February 1934, Sandino was assassinated by members of the National Guard, an American-inspired military force that became the dominant political tool for the elite who ruled Nicaragua for the next four decades. By 1936, political control of Nicaragua was in the hands of Anastasio Somoza. Under Somoza, Nicaragua became almost a caricature of a Southern Hemisphere authoritarian regime, with the predictable concentration of wealth in the hands of a few, total disregard for human rights, brutal repression of even the most temperate efforts aimed at reform, and consistent support from the government of the United States.

In Nicaragua, as elsewhere in Latin America, the American concept of being a "good neighbor" seemed to be based on two related ideas: that the neighborhood should be kept safe from boat rockers no matter how moderate, and that it should be ruled by "strongmen" who would do the bidding of their United States masters. In most places the Catholic church collaborated with this repressive system, as did most of the other institutions in Latin American society.

Nicaraguans made periodic attempts to challenge the unjust status quo, but all reformers were categorized as "subversives" and killed, or otherwise neutralized by the Somoza government. Revolution eventually became the only viable option for those Nicaraguans fed up with Somoza's thuggery.

In 1979 the Somoza dictatorship, which had ruled for forty-five years and was the longest-running "show" in Latin America, was overthrown by an uprising led by the Frente Sandinista de Liberacion Nacional (FSLN), or the Sandinista National Liberation Front. When Somoza fled Nicaragua, he took with him $200 million plundered from the country, and left behind 50,000 dead, 200,000 homeless, 40,000 orphans, and a national debt of over $4 billion (Acker 1986).

For ten years the new Sandinista government struggled to rebuild a country that for decades had been devastated by poverty, illiteracy, and malnutrition. For the first time, new opportunities became available for the vast majority of Nicaraguans, as education and health care became priorities for the new government. One teacher we met put it this way: "Before, child welfare was a matter of charity . . . now it is a matter of social justice."

The Sandinistas built 3,267 schools during their ten-year rule and made education available (at least in principle) for everyone, not just for a privileged few. A literacy campaign begun in 1980 reduced the illiteracy rate from over 50 percent to less than 13 percent (Radinsky 1990). Nicaraguan youth played a crucial role in the literacy campaign. We met a young woman, who, in 1981, when she was only thirteen years old, had gone to live among the peasants to teach them to read and write. She persisted in holding her classes in the local church, even though Contras would disrupt her classes and threaten her and her pupils.

Health care for all was initiated. Hundreds of hospitals and health clinics were built, with poor urban neighborhoods and isolated mountain settlements especially targeted for service (Gannon 1989). By 1986, 24,000 health workers had been trained. Polio was eradicated, and malaria was reduced by 50 percent. Improved health care reduced the infant mortality rate from 120 per 1,000 in 1979 to 57 per 1,000 in 1989 (Radinsky 1990).

Children's mental health care programs, nonexistent before 1979, were started. While professionals with formal credentials were few (1 clinical psychologist per 50,000 people, 1 psychiatrist per 100,000 people, and only 1 child psychiatrst in the whole country [Metraux 1990, 1]), by 1986 more than 20,000 community mental health workers had been trained. These mental health workers would go into communities and teach people how to help children and parents who were experiencing emotional problems, especially the psychological impact of war. Services for special needs children and day care for all children were also established by the Social Security and Welfare Institute. Special schools were established to protect children at high risk and to help those children who were falling behind in schoolwork (Tully 1989).

In one such school in Matagalpa, most of the children have lost their fathers to kidnapping or death. Because of their families' poverty, these children have to earn money, perhaps selling newspapers, shining shoes, or working in the marketplace. Even though most children work six hours a day, many of these children also go to school part-time.

New Homes for the Children of War

Under the Sandinistas, the Nicaraguan government adopted a policy of promoting relocation of children orphaned by the war within their family's home region whenever possible. In addition, the government encouraged local placement with relatives or, if necessary, with foster parents.

Most of the children not placed with local relatives fall into one of two categories: special needs children who require services not available in the countryside (e.g., specialized medical care) or children who have no available local relatives, for whom adequate foster parents are not available, and/or who are in special danger in their home community for political reasons.

Flora, an eight-year-old girl we met, is a typical Nicaraguan child. She lives in a one-room shanty with her mother and siblings. After school she sells candy and cigarettes on the street near the beach along Lake Nicaragua. We asked her how her life is different under current policies from what it would have been before. She replied, "I have food to eat. I can go to school. I can go to the beach." In a country faced with pervasive poverty and a history of pernicious discrimination and exploitation, these are major accomplishments.

However, life has been severely disrupted by more than a decade of war in Nicaragua. The country has been wracked by armed conflict virtually since the inception of its new government. Armed attacks on government and civilian targets by the Contras began in 1980, shortly after the Sandinistas came to power. These attacks intensified in 1981 after former members of Somoza's National Guard formed the Fuerza Democratica Nicaraguense (FDN), the Nicaraguan Democratic Force. The "Guardia" were a ruthless force that worked on Somoza's behalf to destroy his enemies and keep him in power. Their record as "enforcers" on behalf of privilege and repression made them feared and hated by anyone who had a glimmer of sensibility or a breath of sympathy for reform.

The Contras rarely engaged the Sandinista armies in direct military confrontation. They preferred to attack civilians and to spread terror. Because the fighting occurred mainly in rural areas, peasants bore the brunt of these attacks. Their farming suffered because they had to spend time on defense and planning their lives around the eventuality of attack (Gannon 1989). The Contras destroyed bridges, roads, and electrical installations; raided government farms, agricultural cooperatives, and settlements for those displaced by the war; and ambushed vehicles with civilian passengers.

Community leaders, local trade union officials, lay preachers, and young professionals engaged in government-sponsored development and political work in rural areas were singled out for attacks by the Contras as part of a deliberate policy of discouraging collaboration with government agencies. The attacks continued even after a cease-fire was declared in April 1988. As of 1990, more than 30,000 Nicaraguans had been killed (Radinsky 1990).

Civilians were routinely kidnapped during raids, taken to Contra camps, and forcibly recruited into their ranks. According to Amnesty International, thousands of civilians remain unaccounted for, despite persistent efforts by their families to trace them (Amnesty International 1989).

Children suffered alongside adults. One ten-year-old who saw his parents kidnapped by the Contras followed them. He told the Contras he wanted to be with his parents. The Contras told him that they would return with his parents in a few hours and that he should wait for them. He waited for two days in the jungle, alone and without food, but they never returned. He is now responsible for his six younger brothers and sisters (Acker 1986).

We visited a center for orphaned children. These children are vivid reminders of the consequences of war. Juan, a deaf boy whose parents were killed by the Contras, was acting like a dog and eating mud when he arrived. Magdalina, who had been paralyzed since birth, was left in a field to die after her parents were killed by Contras. Carlos, who was epileptic, was found roaming the countryside after his parents were killed.

More than 150,000 children have been displaced from their homes. As of 1987, at least 455 children under age fifteen had been killed and 691 were missing. Some 1,542 children under age fifteen had been wounded, as had 1,865 youth aged fifteen to twenty (Nelson 1989).

In rural areas it has become common to see small children who have lost arms and legs, the result of encounters with buried land mines. Ten-year-old Alfredo and his five-year-old brother Bayardo were injured when they uncovered a buried land mine while playing in a field near their home. Their bodies were burned and scarred, and it is likely that they will never see again (Kinzer 1988). While this mine was apparently placed by retreating Contras to prevent Sandinista soldiers from following them, children have also been injured by land mines that Sandinistas plant to prevent Contra attacks. Eleven-year-old Josefa's leg was blown off by one such mine as she was walking near an electric plant near the city of Jinotega (Kinzer 1989).

Children's homes are not safe havens from this random terror. Grenades have been thrown into homes, causing injury and death to children. Twelve-year-old Casimiro and his younger brother were at home with their mother when a fragmentation grenade exploded in their home. While no one knows whether the grenade was fired by the Contras attacking their farm cooperative or by the Sandinistas defending it, what is clear is that this mother and her two children were critically injured. Casimiro's face is disfigured from the shrapnel, and he is blinded in one eye. While a prosthetic ankle joint would enable him to walk again, such a device is not available in Nicaragua. From his hospital bed he declares, "I'm getting ready to leave the hospital, but I only want to go somewhere that's safe" (Kinzer 1988).

The years of conflict have exacerbated the child welfare challenge on both the supply and the demand sides. Nicaragua is suffering from a resource crisis: despite a dramatic increase in the number of children who need assistance, the country doesn't have enough resources to cope with the problem. The fighting has also taken its toll on the initial gains made in education and health. The illiteracy rate, which had decreased from over 50 percent to 13 percent, had risen to 25 percent by 1989. More than 400 teachers have been killed and 640 schools destroyed by the Contras, depriving thousands of children of education (Gannon 1989).

An embargo by the United States has severely affected Nicaragua's economy, and thus the welfare of its population. Inflation had risen 34,000 percent by 1989 (Robinson and Speck 1990, 40). By 1990, there was often no bread, rice, meat, and milk on the shelves in the stores. Even when these items were available, most people could not afford them.

As a result of these shortages, malnutrition has increased. It is estimated that 80 percent of Nicaragua's children were malnourished in 1989 (McMullen 1990, 9). Infectious diseases are also on the rise. In 1990 more than 1,300 children died from measles, diarrhea, dengue fever, and other infections (Cockburn 1990, 586–587). Because of shrinking resources, the government has had to close day care centers. Many that remain open often do not have milk or food for the children.

Additionally, the mental health of children has suffered. As many as 50,000 children have suffered psychological trauma because they have lost their homes, been attacked, suffered kidnapping and abuse, been injured, or lost parents, siblings, relatives, or friends to the violence (Nelson 1989). A study by Metraux found that children living in areas in which heavy fighting occurred had more than twice the negative psychological symptoms as children living in relatively safer areas (Metraux 1988).

An indirect effect of the war is that more children are being abandoned and abused. Parents, especially single mothers, are unable to feed or care for their children because of dire economic conditions. Two-year-old Maria was abandoned by her mother when she was nine months old after her father was killed in the war. She was fortunate because her grandmother took her to live with her and nine aunts, uncles, and cousins in a one-room, dirt-floor shack. Other children who do not have relatives who can care for them reside at centers for abandoned and abused children.

A severe housing shortage has occurred as people have fled the fighting in the countryside for the safety of Managua. Because so many men are serving in the army have been kidnapped or killed, women and their children have come to Managua in search of work and a better life. Because of the war, roughly 60 percent of Nicaraguans now live in Managua instead of the 35 percent who lived there in 1980. Housing is prohibitively expensive, and consequently out of the range of the majority of the population. In Nicaragua, as elsewhere in the world, war means excessive urbanization in a country that lacks the urban infrastructure to support this pattern of growth.

Even before the war Managua suffered a housing crisis. An earthquake in 1972 devastated much of the city: 5,000 people were killed, and 250,000 homes were destroyed. Eighteen years later many of the remaining buildings still looked bombed out. We saw families living in these crumbling, abandoned buildings. Thousands of other families live in one-room shacks, made of tin, plastic, or cardboard, with no electricity or running water.

During our visit in 1990, 500 one-room shacks were being built by their future inhabitants in a field next to the United States embassy and within sight of the ambassador's hillside mansion. This is an irony not lost on anyone familiar with the U.S. government's role in producing the current situation. A man we talked to about this new housing site described these people as the lucky ones. He said that many others are worse off, living in even more crowded conditions.

We visited Nicaragua after the February 1990 elections in which Sandinista Daniel Ortega was defeated by the National Opposition Union (UNO) candidate Violeta Chamorro. Many of the people we talked to told us that while in their hearts they supported the Sandinistas, they nevertheless voted for Chamorro because they felt that they had no choice. They knew the United States would only withdraw the Contras and end the embargo on food if Chamorro won. For ten years the people had suffered the ravages of U.S. low-intensity warfare. They wanted the killing to stop. They did not want their children to starve anymore. Was this the only reason the Sandinistas lost the election to the UNO coalition? Probably not.

We heard frequent charges of government corruption and misman-agement. Ortega's party is certainly not blameless when it comes to toting up the crimes committed against Nicaragua in the last ten years. But for anyone with sympathies for children and their needs and their rights, the horrible question is this: how much better would Nicaragua have become under the Sandinistas if they had been accepted by the United States, rather than attacked and thwarted? What if the Reagan administration had not decided in 1981 to arm and finance the remnants of Somoza's National Guard and to trans-form it into a "Contra" rebel force? What if there had been no U.S. economic embargo against Nicaragua?

This is what the politics of suffering are really about: making chil-dren pay in the name of some "higher purpose." Supporters of the Contras and those more commoly labeled terrorists who capture and massacre children to "send a message" to their enemies are bed-fellows in the same sleazy room.

A Little Girl's Story

Candida grew up on a *finca,* a farm in the country with trees, cows, and chickens. For several years fighting had been occurring in her region. After some of the teenagers in the region were kidnapped by Contras, Candida's father sent some of his older children to live in another village that was safer. One day, when Candida was nine years old, she went out with her father and mother to milk the cows. A group of Contras ambushed and kidnapped all three of them. Candida was separated from her parents and taken away by the Contras. She was held hostage for five months during which time she learned the Contra life: stealing food from houses and carrying supplies while the Contras moved about.

She shuddered as she told us about being forced to watch as the Contras stripped a kidnapped man naked, and then slit his throat with a knife. Afterward, she was given his clothes to wear.

Some of the Contras tried to rape her. An older Contra inter-vened, claiming that she already belonged to him. He kept her as his "mascot" and protected her from the others. Candida stated that two other kidnapped girls with her had not been so lucky. One was chosen to be the "wife" of the leader, and the other girl was communally raped. She told us, "Every day I prayed I would survive just one more day." Our tax money paid for all this.

After she had been with the Contras for three months, she met a teacher from her region who had also been kidnapped. From her Candida learned of her parents' fate. Candida wept as she told us that her brother had searched for them for three days before he found their decomposed bodies. They had been murdered by the Contras after Candida was taken from them.

When the Contras were crossing the border to Honduras, they left Candida to work at a Contra sympathizer's house. She considered herself lucky because "usually they kill the people they don't take across." She was later able to escape from the house.

Her reunion with the rest of her family was brief. The Contras knew she had escaped and were looking for her. She had to go into hiding with an aunt from another region for three months, and eventually had to leave the region because it was not safe there either. Candida and three of her sisters were taken to an orphanage near Managua.

Candida was adopted by an "aunt," the cousin of her father. Her aunt described how Candida would not talk the first year. She had nightmares. She would fall out of bed at night. During the day she was fearful and anxious.

Sixteen now, she is known as the *solidad,* the one who is not yet married. She told us she had more important things on her agenda. Sure, she has boyfriends, but she plans to become a civil engineer. She excels in school, especially at math, and has finished six grades in less than three years. She had the opportunity to study abroad—government policy dictates that war orphans are entitled to the best education—but she preferred to study in Nicaragua and stay with her family. She is very active in politics and is very proud that she could vote in the elections. While she hopes there won't be more war, she will join the struggle if necessary.

Like some of the survivors of war trauma we have met in other countries, Candida seems to want to make her life into a statement. Those who have survived and suffered sometimes seem driven to make their lives count, to achieve as an affirmation that their very existence is a testimony to something of higher value. We were moved by this phenomenon and returned home with a finer appreciation of how some fellow humans take a kind of positive revenge on those who made them confront the dark side of human experience. But we must never forget that these specialists in human survival bear heavy emotional burdens, burdens that take their toll in the dark of the night and in the early morning hours when memory rules. Years later, the now-adult Candidas of the world often show the psychic wear and tear of their triumph.

We also talked with three of Candida's sisters, Rosa Yasmina, age nine, Arelis, age twelve, and Alba, age fourteen, who were at the orphanage with her and are now living with different adoptive and foster parents in Managua.

Rosa Jasmina now lives with her adoptive parents in a one-room house in Managua. At first she said she did not remember her parents because she was so young. But as she talked with us, her painful memories emerged. She remembered that neighbors warned her father that the Contras would kill him. She remembered being afraid and hiding. She told us about having to leave her parents to stay with her godmother in another town so that she would be safe. She cried as she remembered her godmother telling her that her parents had been murdered.

Arelis lives comfortably with her foster parents and their children in a large house in Managua. While talking to us about her life now, she spoke in the educated style of the city, but when talking about her childhood, she switched back to a country dialect. She could not remember a time when the Contras were not around. She told us she was always afraid. Arelis recognized some of the Contras who were former neighbors even though they would hide their faces behind handkerchiefs when they came to her house demanding food. She remembered her father and mother being threatened. On one occasion they tied her brother up, and later did the same thing to her father. She remembered trying to escape one time—her mother preparing food for a journey, the family sneaking out at night, then being found by the Contras and being forced to return to their house.

Alba's most distinct memory concerns the day her parents and sister never returned. She and her brothers and sisters were on their own for three days before their brother found their murdered parents and got help. Alba saw the bodies of her parents before they were buried. Because the bodies were decomposed, the family could not get permission to bury them in the cemetery, and so they buried them in their *finca*.

She could not understand why the Contras would kill her father: "He was not political." She has already learned to give expression to "the just-world hypothesis" to which most of us cling, the belief that there must always be a reason for what happens, that the world is orderly, that there is always something one could or should do to be safe. Would that it were so.

We asked Alba what her hopes and dreams were. Alba hoped the Contras would disarm. She wanted the fighting to end. She also hoped that someday when she is older she can live together with all her sisters. Her dream is for her and the older sisters to work, have their own house, and look after the smaller children. When she grows up she wants to be "a doctor who cares for children and old people." How often we have heard this or a similar desire from children seeking to integrate the horror of their experiences with the hope in their hearts. Unfortunately, we have heard this mostly from girls. From boys we more often hear that they wish to be soldiers to avenge their lost ones through violence.

We also asked Alba what should be done to the Contras who had killed her parents. "Some say they should do to them what they did to my parents. I say they should just go back to their own families and stop all the killing and that's it. Just stop it." Thank heaven for little girls.

"Here Nobody Surrenders"

So read the sign as we crossed the bridge into Matagalpa, a city with a population of 70,000, divided into six barrios. It has experienced much fighting. Electricity has been sabotaged, food stores have been robbed, and many civilians have been attacked.

One of the barrios we visited in Matagalpa is called the Heroes and Martyrs of Gautes Mendosa. The largest and best organized, it is a resettlement area composed largely of women and children. Their husbands and fathers have been killed during the fighting.

Two-year-old Maria lives here with her grandmother, aunts, uncles, and cousins. All nine occupy a one-room tin shanty with a dirt floor. A picture of Maria's father hangs on the wall. When she was only three days old, her seventeen-year-old father was killed in a Contra ambush.

Maria's aunt works at the local day care center. The thirty-eight children in her center, aged two months to three years, were displaced by the war; their fathers have been kidnapped, seriously wounded, or killed.

That the Sandinistas have this problem to address, and that they have chosen to do so in this way, is emblematic of the story of Nicaragua. And it is why progressive professionals from around the world have been coming to Nicaragua for the last decade to help. Like the Spanish Civil War of the 1930s, the Sandinista-Contra civil war has been a kind of political litmus test. Regarding Nicaragua, you are forced to choose, not between the "Good Guys" and the "Bad Guys," but between the "Guys Who Basically Have the Right Idea in Contrast to the Bad Guys of the Past" and the "Guys Who Either Were the Bad Guys in the Past or Who Are in It for the Wrong Reasons (Plus Some Guys Who Unfortunately Ended Up on the Wrong Side as a Nasty By-product of the Less Than Perfect Way the Better Guys Went About Trying to Overthrow the Bad Guys)." It is often less morally satisfying than a choice between the absolute Good Guys and the absolute Bad Guys.

When the day care center we visited in Matagalpa was first started, the children always had at least corn to eat and milk to drink. Today the center often has neither to offer. The children are given weak tea, and sometimes a piece of bread. Many of the children are malnourished. Sometimes there is no money to pay the salaries of the two staff members.

Even after moving out of the "war zone" to this safer resettlement area, Maria's grandmother is still fearful. "I can't feel safe when no one knows what will happen, when the next attack will be." She does not let her grandchildren out of her sight outside for fear they will be hurt.

A Mother's Story

Ana is one of the mothers living in the barrio of Heroes and Martyrs. She was originally from the northern region of Kual, but fled to Matagalpa because her family was in danger. First, the Contras had burned a coffee storehouse that her family owned. Next, they kidnapped one of her sons while he was picking coffee. Even though a religious organization intervened to free her son, she is still shaken by the experience. "Why would they do these things?" Ana asked us. "We are working people."

Another time, a group of Contras came at night while Ana and her children were sleeping. They took food and supplies and the machete they used for working in the fields. Then they forced three of her sons to go with them, telling them they would recruit them into their army.

The Contras also kidnapped sixty other young boys from Ana's town and conscripted them. Her three sons and two of her neighbor's children escaped after eleven days and returned to their village. A few days later, Contras came and killed the two neighbor boys in their home. Fearing for her own and her sons' lives, she fled to Jinotega, where some relatives lived, and then came to Matagalpa because Jinotega was also too close to the fighting.

Children as Leaders

The children and youth we talked to hope there isn't more war. One young girl told us, "We don't want war. I don't think children *anywhere* want war." However, they are willing to take up arms and fight. Brenda, age fifteen, exemplifies this spirit:

> There was a fiesta in the village. . . . A peasant ran into the dance to say a large band of Contras was coming. . . . Eight of us kids in the militia managed to get the children and the old people into some trenches we had dug. But there were about a hundred armed Contras, and we weren't very good at fighting. We kept on shooting for hours, but there were too many of them and they overran us. All my friends were killed. They shot me twice in the legs and in my right arm. I fell beside the others, but I could still see. The Contras came up, and they began to cut the heads off my friends, and I was terrified they would do the same with me. But one of the Contras started shouting that the Nicaraguan army was coming, so they all fled. The army got me to hospital, but it was too late to save my right arm. My legs were not badly damaged, but they had to cut off the arm at the shoulder.

Brenda learned how to write and type with her left hand. Now she works for the Sandinista Youth Organization, organizing children's

events, radio programs, and publications. "The Association of Sandinista Children (ANS) wasn't just formed *for* children. It was
formed *by* children. They had fought in the revolution . . . and they
were not going to let anybody keep them out" (Acker 1986).

Nicaragua's Organization of the Revolutionary Disabled (ORD)
was founded by a youth whose spinal column was severed by a bullet from Somoza's National Guard as he tried to rescue some children who had been shot during the fighting of the revolution. There
are over 600 members, all disabled, mainly from the revolution.
Known as "wheelchair revolutionaries," the youth counsel, instruct,
and help find work for 10,000 other disabled people. They also
make wheelchairs for themselves and for other disabled people from
bicycle wheels brought in by sympathetic donors from the United
States (Acker 1986).

The Contras Are "Made in the U.S.A."

Since the Sandinista government came to power, the United States
government has used military, economic, and political means to
ensure that they would not succeed. Many conservative Americans
believed that the Sandinistas represented a threat to the interests
of the United States. They threatened "our" commercial interests.
Recall that in Chile our government and some influential corporate
friends financed and stimulated the overthrow of Salvadore Allende's
elected revolutionary government. The success of the Sandinistas
conjured up the prospect of "another Cuba." Our national identity
is wrapped up in part in remembering such affronts to our Manifest
Destiny. Beyond that is the broader sense of the Monroe Doctrine:
we are benificent "patrons" of this hemisphere, and anyone ungrate-
ful enough to dispute that should be punished. Add to this the legitimate concerns of democrats in Nicaragua and elsewhere that the
program of revolutionary change under the Sandinistas was prone
to excesses and bad judgments.

The result of all this was that the Contra forces received money,
arms, other supplies, military training, and operational guidance
from the CIA and other United States government agencies until
1988 (after which they still received official nonmilitary, "humanitarian" assistance and also continued to be supplied militarily
through the efforts of various covert and private sources).

The CIA was responsible for attacking ships in Nicaraguan ports, organizing sabotage attacks on oil installations and power plants, and having the Managua airport bombed. United States military aid to the Contras has contributed to numerous abuses of human rights, including torture and executions, according to Amnesty International (1989). This can hardly be news to anyone who reads the newspaper.

Just as there is always a new crop of war criminals to do the dirty work, there is never any shortage of "good Germans" who are willing to look the other way and fail to know, as did millions of normal and decent German citizens during the Nazi era. And the mix of war criminals seeking some final solution to the problems of an imperfect world and a complicitous citizenry always means orphaned and frightened children, lost limbs and parents, nightmares and vows of revenge. With business as usual, we could spend the rest of our lives visiting war zones to hear from children who have lived the politics of suffering.

We left Nicaragua on the eve of the Sandinistas' surrender of formal political power to the UNO coalition. Violeta Chamorro was about to be inaugurated as president. The country seemed to be on the verge of economic disaster. The water workers were on strike. The banks were on strike. Gasoline had run out. International telephone communication was suspended. The UN peacekeeping forces had arrived to oversee the political transition. One peacekeeper told us he was skeptical that the transition would be smooth because the Contras were unwilling to give up their arms and the Sandinistas were unwilling to give up their power. All seemed uncertain. Would the Contras lay down their weapons? Would the Sandinistas hand over their control of the government? Would the civil war really end? Would the United States make amends?

In the months following Chamorro's inauguration, the new government has had to contend with a crumbling infrastructure, widespread hunger, and unemployment reaching 40 percent (Sheppard 1990). The cordoba, the national monetary unit, was devalued thirty-five times in 1990, making survival almost impossible. For example, the monthly electricity bill for a lower-middle-class family in April 1990 was $.91. By July 1990 it was $37.80—more than a teacher's monthly salary (Cockburn 1990, 586–587).

The political turmoil rages on. Many of Chamorro's former supporters, including ex-Contras, have staged violent protests, demanding the changes that were to accompany free enterprise and democracy. While 16,000 Contras had been demobilized and returned to civilian life in exchange for farmland and $30 million in U.S. aid, the government has lagged behind in its resettlement program, and violent land disputes have erupted between ex-Contras and Sandinista civilians.

In July 1990 a Sandinista labor federation staged a violent general strike that paralyzed Managua and brought the country to the edge of civil war again as armed Sandinistas fought government forces. Four people were killed and scores injured. In September the new government laid off 15,000 government workers. In October 1990 the conflict escalated when four ex-Contras were killed trying to reclaim land from a Sandinista-run agricultural cooperative near the town of San Juan del Rio Coco. As a result, protesters blocked roads, seized police stations, and occupied town halls. When this round of fighting stopped, twelve people lay dead and dozens more were injured (Lane and Padgett 1990).

We were asked by a young girl we met, whose brother had been killed and who herself had been displaced from her home, why our country allowed such things to happen. After seeing the destruction, the random terror that has resulted from United States intervention in the internal politics of Nicaragua, we too must ask, "Why?"

6

Palestinians in Revolt:

Children of the Intifada

Amidst the squalor of the refugee camp, Fedwa is an oasis of sweet intelligence. At eleven, she is the oldest of seven or eight children—it's hard to be sure which of the mob of boys and girls around us are her siblings and which are cousins or neighbors. She is clearly the "little mother," however, and in an earlier conversation she had told us that she wants to be a physician when she grows up. Now she sings us a song she has written. Her voice is clear and strong, but still a child's voice, as she sings these words:

> Our life is oppression and tribulation.
> Although this child's blood is spent,
> It is not in vain.
> The *Intifada* continues, and the youth are awakening.
> The coming generation, oh Palestine,
> Will one day be free.

Fedwa is a charming child *and* a committed patriot, a "little mother" to her siblings *and* a "soldier" in the front ranks of a popular uprising. She is a Palestinian, a child of the *Intifada*.

Where Is Palestine?

Fedwa's life says a great deal about her generation and her people. She lives . . . where? Even the simple act of naming the place where she lives is a hotly contested issue; it makes our discussion of her life intrinsically and inescapably "political" and "controversial." *She* would say that she lives "in Palestine," or perhaps "in occupied Palestine." Other people would say that Fedwa lives in the "West Bank" or in "the Occupied Territories." Many Israelis would say that she lives in "Samaria" (the sister province to "Judea") and others that she lives in "the Administered Territories." The choice of words for Palestinians and Israelis is significant. The nuances may be lost on an outsider, but they are potent for everyone who must live with the implications and the consequences of these word choices.

We will call her a Palestinian, and the place where she lives "the West Bank," in the interest of moving forward with our discussion of her life in a war zone. Not that we really can do so and avoid being "political." After the Palestine Liberation Organization (PLO) declared the existence of a Palestinian state in this area in November 1988 more than ninety nations recognized the PLO as the government of this "Palestine." Those that did not based their decision in part upon the principle that a government must control some territory to claim official recognition. While the Israelis are not fully in control in Fedwa's "hometown," the PLO is not the government "on the ground" except in a very indirect and covert way, perhaps as a shadow government existing alongside the official Israeli system of occupation.

Whatever we call the place where Fedwa lives, her family has no political rights: displaying the Palestinian flag is considered a "terrorist" act and is subject to punishment. Even wearing the colors of the Palestinian flag is illegal. The government around her is the Israeli military. Anyone who visits Fedwa's homeland can discover this firsthand.

On one visit we stopped in a nearby town to watch Israeli soldiers as they forced shops to open that had closed as part of a commercial strike. When the local commander discovered our presence, he ordered us out of the town and prohibited pictures. "How can you do this?" we asked. "I am the law here," he said. Sitting in his jeep surrounded by heavily armed colleagues, his point of view had a cold logic. Of course our American passports provided some protection from his "law," but an angry armed soldier usually gets his way—at least for the moment.

We could always move on, even go home. Fedwa's family lives in a refugee camp, *chooses* to live here, rather than abandon their idea of a Palestinian "homeland" and move somewhere else as many Israelis would like them to do (and as hundreds of thousands of other Palestinians have done). An Israeli military observation post sits on top of a hill overlooking the refugee camp. Fedwa walks to school under the eyes of the soldiers. She has been detained on her way to school by soldiers, and soldiers have broken into her home in the refugee camp in the middle of the night looking for someone to arrest. Such is life under the occupation.

Fedwa is poor by our standards. She and her large family live in two rooms—and the alley beyond. Why does her family remain in the camp? In part, it is a matter of economic necessity; in part, it is a political statement. She and many other Palestinians believe that if they were to leave for another country they would be abandoning "the cause," giving up their claim to "the Palestinian homeland." Their presence in the camps is a "fact on the ground," a statement: we exist, we have a *home*, and we wait to return to it.

To an outsider, Fedwa's situation seems grim, even hopeless. But she has hope—she writes poems and songs about having her own country someday. She does have a childhood in many important ways. She and her friends play in the alleys. She reads. She helps her mother. She shows her schoolwork to her father, who is himself a teacher. She smiles. She dreams.

And she is actively involved in trying to change her situation. She participates in demonstrations to protest the occupation. She studies hard, even when her school is closed down by the military authorities, so that she can fulfill her dream of becoming a doctor. She tells us that when the schools were closed, she held a class for the younger children in her home. This was illegal: adult teachers who organized such alternate schools were threatened with having their houses demolished. In January 1990 she went back to school, when the Israeli authorities permitted the reopening of the schools after nearly two years of closure. We visited her there, in her math class. She is a good student, her teacher tells us, and it is easy to believe her.

Children Living between a Rock and a Hard Place

Fedwa is one of nearly 900,000 Palestinian children living in the West Bank and Gaza Strip; these children make up more than 60 percent of the population there. They have grown up with the military occupation and political struggle, and all that it means for day-to-day life and for their concept of the future.

Sometimes resistance to the occupation has been "on the back burner." Sometimes it has flared up. For the last three years it has been boiling over in what is called "the *Intifada.*" The *Intifada* literally means "a shaking off" in Arabic. It is a special kind of war, a popular Uprising by Palestinians against Israeli occupation. It began in December 1987, after an incident in the Gaza Strip when an Israeli truck collided with a taxi and killed four Palestinians. In the ensuing days, Palestinians revolted, staging a series of demonstrations (some would call them "riots") in the West Bank and Gaza Strip. These demonstrations were followed by a more coordinated program of general strikes and violent protests, acts of mass civil disobedience, and rock throwing. For many of those familiar with the situation, what was surprising was not that the Uprising occurred, but that it had not occurred much earlier.

Israel has occupied the West Bank and Gaza Strip for more than twenty years, ever since the 1967 war. Like everything else in the Middle East, the circumstances of that war—who wanted it, who started it, who caused it—are disputed. What is clear is that after the Jordanians entered the war against Israel, the Israelis drove out the Jordanians, who had occupied the region since Jordan's boundaries became defined through the same 1948 war during which Israel itself became a nation. The Gaza Strip was occupied by Egypt until the 1967 war, when it too fell to the Israelis.

Fedwa's grandparents fled or were driven out of what is now Israel in the 1948 war, and moved eastward, ending up in the refugee camp where she lives today. Twenty-three years have passed since this camp passed out of Jordanian control and into Israeli control. It has never been under the control of a Palestinian state. One might ask if Israeli occupation is better than Jordanian occupation.

Although the Israelis provided a source of jobs inside Israel, and offered some social services, they did this while running their occupation at a profit—taking in more in tax revenues than was spent in services. But the clash of ethnic groups and identities is much stronger and clearer between the Palestinians and the Israelis than it was between the Palestinians and the Jordanians (many of whom share a religious and ethnic heritage). Moreover, the Israelis have seized land and generally have tried to displace the Palestinians in the West Bank while building a network of more than one hundred settlements. They have also officially annexed East Jerusalem and have begun to settle there as well.

For more than forty years these Palestinians have been refugees who live just a few hours' driving distance away from what had been their own land for generations. Many times if you ask a child in the refugee camps "Where do you live?" he or she responds with the name of one of the approximately four hundred villages that existed before the 1948 war and is now either erased or converted into an Israeli (Jewish) town. Home is a memory and a concept. It is difficult for a child to understand this. Adults pretend to understand.

Living in a Land Dominated by Histories

Many histories are at work in the Middle East. Palestinian children and youth are simultaneously the embodiment of the past and the prospect for the future. Having lived under military occupation their entire lives, many seem to believe that the time has arrived to assert themselves and redeem their "honor." Their choice of weapons has proved to be astute.

The world's mass media has conveyed the almost unavoidable "David and Goliath" imagery: Palestinian youths armed with stones confronting Israeli soldiers who respond by firing back with potentially lethal rubber bullets, tear gas grenades, and live ammunition. One American analyst, a specialist in nonviolent resistance, has concluded that the *Intifada* has been about 80 percent nonviolent (protests, strikes, symbolic acts, civil disobedience) and believes that if it were 100 percent nonviolent it would succeed more quickly (Sharp 1989). That advice does not fall on fertile soil in many cases, and the possibility of violent escalation is always present in the *Intifada* (and indeed did increase in the last few months of 1990 in the wake of Israeli forces killing at least seventeen Palestinians in an incident at the Temple Mount/Haram al-Sharif in Jerusalem). As hopes for peace decline, the prospect of heightened violence increases.

Political violence is not new to Palestinians; the whole region is steeped in it. One need only walk through Jerusalem to have a feeling for the political and military conflict that has swirled around this city of holy places. Innumerable ancient peoples, the

Israelites, the Romans, the Crusaders, the Ottoman Empire, and modern states have fought over this land again and again.

And we must not forget that the Zionist movement that led to the creation of Israel was itself steeped in political violence. The anti-Semitic pogroms directed at European Jewry stimulated aggressive efforts to reclaim the ancient Jewish homeland. Anti-Jewish violence in Palestine resulted in a militant and military Zionist movement to protect Jewish settlement interests. Killings and bombings were tactics commonly employed against the British authorities who controlled the government of Palestine. Indeed, many of the older generation of Israeli political leaders were labeled "terrorists" when they sought to make space for the country they hoped to build. As one wag put it, "A terrorist becomes a statesman if he wins."

Before World War I, the territory now called Palestine was part of the Ottoman Empire, as it had been for five centuries. In 1917 Palestine was conquered by British imperial forces led by General Allenby and "liberated" from Ottoman control. British domination of Palestine was subsequently sanctioned by the League of Nations through the mandate system. Britain had also promised to set aside a portion of Palestine as a "national home" for the Jews of Europe (and a place in which the Jews already present could find political ascendancy).

What gave the British government the right to make such a commitment? That is what colonial powers do, isn't it? They make decisions about the fate of other places and peoples. Americans ought to be able to understand that phenomenon—and how those "other places and peoples" feel about it.

Zionist forces fought the British in a long campaign of guerilla attacks in the 1930s and 1940s to stimulate progress on the question of a Jewish homeland. At the same time, Palestinians also took up arms to defend their right to self-determination, most notably in an uprising against the British that lasted from 1936 to 1939. We should be able to sympathize with these efforts. After all, was not the *American* Revolution a "shaking off," an "intifada" of its own, based in large measure on a desire to enable Americans to control the fate of America—never mind the Indians and slaves.

British rule in Palestine from 1917 to 1947 was marked by unsuccessful attempts to manage the growing conflict between the Arab inhabitants and the European Jewish immigrants to these territories who came to join the Jews still there nearly two thousand years after the Diaspora. They came to escape anti-Semitism or to fulfill their Zionist dreams of a safe and holy place to reconstitute themselves, their history, and their religious mission. The rise of Nazism in Germany and the Holocaust it wrought stimulated large-scale Jewish movement to Palestine. The Jews saw themselves as "coming home" to their ancient roots; the Arabs saw this same movement as just another colonial invasion. Both groups still hold fast to these radically divergent interpretations.

After World War II violence escalated dramatically, and attacks against the British "occupation" by Jewish terrorist/freedom fighters increased. In 1947 the British government announced its decision to terminate its mandate, evacuate Palestine, and refer the matter to the United Nations. In accordance with a plan drawn up by its special Committee on Palestine, the United Nations voted to partition the area into separate Arab and Jewish states in November 1947.

Zionist Jews in Palestine saw this plan as a good vehicle for realizing their aspirations and accepted it. Some Jews who argued for a secular, binational state opposed it (and in some cases went to jail for their opposition). Most Arabs saw the plan as a defeat and argued that it gave the Zionists much more land than their numbers warranted. Some Arabs resigned themselves to the "two-state solution." Not surprisingly, intercommunal warfare broke out in the winter of 1947.

The massacre of over 250 Palestinian villagers in Deir Yassin in April 1948 by Israeli forces played a decisive role in inducing other Palestinians to flee their homes. Unable to return to their homes, many Palestinians were settled in refugee camps. These events are known to Palestinians as the *Nakba,* "the Catastrophe," and the Palestinians of the 1948–49 refugee camps and their descendants, especially those in the West Bank and the Gaza Strip—numbering about 850,000 today—form the core of the Palestinian-Israeli problem.

When Israel declared its independence in May 1948, the disputed area was invaded by the armies of five Arab states. During the ensuing hostilities that continued intermittently until July 1949, Israel triumphed, but at a high cost: 1 percent of the entire Jewish population died. Arab casualties numbered in the tens of thousands, and between 770,000 and 780,000 Palestinians (from a population of 1,400,000—more than half the population) were displaced from areas that came under Israeli control (Abu-Lughod 1971).

The situation was further complicated by the Six Day War in June 1967. Not only did additional Palestinians become refugees as a result of the Israeli seizure of the West Bank from Jordan and the Gaza Strip from Egypt, but all of Arab East Jerusalem was formally annexed to Israel. From 1948 to 1968, Israel confiscated almost 250,000 acres of land from Palestinians to make room for Jewish settlers. Since 1968, the process of Jewish settlement has continued throughout the West Bank and, to a lesser extent, in the Gaza Strip.

In the minds and hearts of many Palestinians—even those who were born long after the events themselves—"home" is a spot inside the Jewish State of Israel, a spot to which they are prohibited from returning, a spot in which they are now officially unwanted and illegal "aliens." No matter where one stands in sorting out the competing historical claims and counterclaims, one ought to be able to understand the anger, the pain, and the memories that live on in the elders who remember, and the succeeding generations who are taught to remember, feelings and memories that are often encouraged and used for political purposes.

The *Intifada*

The *Intifada* is an intensification and institutionalization of the conflict that has existed for decades. First described as an event in December 1987, the Uprising has now become a condition of life for virtually all Palestinian children and youth. Nearly all families and villages are touched directly by the ongoing crises associated with the Uprising, although variation in intensity exists.

Researchers conducting a study in the West Bank in 1989 were unable to find any children in some towns and cities who had had no direct experience with violence—who had not been shot, detained, arrested, beaten, or teargassed. There *is* variation in the intensity of the conflict. Some communities are characteristically "hotter" than others. Nablus is a prime example of the hot; Jericho of the warm. Nonetheless, there is a sense in which the *Intifada* has become the dominant process for defining day-to-day life as well as the meaning of the future for Palestinians. Consider the case of a little girl named Nur.

Nur is five years old and lives with her eight brothers and sisters, her mother, and her grandmother in a two-room house in Deheisha refugee camp near Bethlehem. The furnishings are sparse: an old couch in one room, a small table with a few broken chairs in the other. On the wall hangs a picture of the children's father.

The last time Nur saw her father was a year ago when she was four. She had been playing with her brothers and sisters in one of the rooms when soldiers began throwing tear gas canisters at demonstrators in the street outside their home. After cautioning the children not to go outside while the soldiers were in the street, their father kept watch by the window. As he looked out the window, a bullet was fired through the window, striking him in the head. This is the last image Nur has of her father.

Later that evening, while the family was mourning, soldiers entered their home and smashed the few belongings the family had, including the photograph of the father. As the soldiers left, they tossed a canister of tear gas into the house.

Nur doesn't talk much. She is fearful and anxious. She doesn't sleep well. Sometimes she dreams her father is coming in a car to take her and her family away from where they now live. Other times she has nightmares about the soldiers shooting her father; she wakes up screaming.

The soldiers continue to come into her home during the night. Twice before they took two of her brothers away at night and beat them in an attempt to get information about their neighbors. The mother reports that Nur is terrified of the soldiers. In spite of her terror, one time she confronted the soldiers when they entered her home, saying, "You killed my father." They responded by pushing her down the steps to the door. When we asked Nur to draw a picture of where she lives, she drew her house surrounded by soldiers shooting at her and her family inside.

A Nation of Children

The total population of Israel and the Occupied Territories is approximately 6 million. Roughly 1.6 million Palestinians live in the Occupied Territories—900,000 in the West Bank and 700,000 in the Gaza Strip. Another 650,000 Palestinians live in Israel and are Israeli citizens, while approximately 140,000 Palestinians live in annexed East Jerusalem. Some 3.5 million Israeli Jews live in Israel, and 70,000 Jewish settlers are living in the Occupied Territories.

Currently, approximately 900,000 Palestinian children sixteen years of age and younger live in the Occupied Territories of the West Bank and Gaza Strip. Some 500,000 of these children live in villages, cities, and refugee camps in the West Bank, an area of 2,847 square miles enclosed by Israel on the north, west, and south, and bounded by the Jordan River on the east. The other 400,000 children live in the Gaza Strip, a piece of land twenty-eight miles long and five miles wide, bounded by Egypt in the south, the Mediterranean Sea in the west, and Israel in the east and north. The Gaza Strip is the most densely populated nonurban area in the world. Though Palestinian refugees were initially housed in what were supposed to be temporary facilities in 1948, a third generation is now growing up in these refugee camps.

Refugee children growing up in the Occupied Territories have suffered from crowded housing, marginal health care, and inadequate school facilities. It is not uncommon for an extended family of twelve or more members to be confined to two small, sparsely furnished rooms. The Israeli authorities have forbidden refugees to add to these dwellings without permission, which is seldom granted.

Health conditions in these refugee camps are often appalling. Many of the camps lack sufficient drinking water, and sewage systems are inadequate or nonexistent. In the Gaza Strip's Jabalya camp, children play in a cesspool that festers with disease. As a result, preventable diseases such as hepatitis and trachoma are rampant. In some parts of the Gaza Strip, infant mortality rates are as high as 100 per 1,000 (UNWRA 1987). Children's education has also suffered. Schools in the camps are overcrowded, and there are not enough books, pencils, or paper for the students.

To Make an Omelet You Have to Break Some Eggs?

Since the Uprising, conditions for Palestinian children have worsened. Even in this very limited war, in which both sides have abided by some unwritten rules most of the time, children suffer indignities and threats to their development. No high-flying strategic bombers are at work here as in Cambodia. Massacres on the scale of Mozambique do not occur. Nonetheless, the costs to children are high.

How does one evaluate the conduct of one nation occupying another? In one sense, there is the absolute scale embodied in the concept of "childhood" as we use that term. Children have an absolute claim to protection, to nurturance, to safety, to discovering their self-worth. But we must also be aware of historical and geographic standards: what is the norm here and now? In the Middle East, the norm is rather brutal.

Consider the pillage of Kuwait by Iraqi forces in 1990–1991: looting, capricious executions, and rape were commonplace. Or consider that the Syrian government's response to a rebellion led by Muslim fundamentalists was to bombard and ultimately completely level an entire city, causing tens of thousands of deaths. Recall that the Saudis killed hundreds of unruly pilgrims in Mecca in an ugly incident less than ten years ago. And remember that the Iraqis responded to Kurdish rebellion by using poison gas to massacre whole villages. Both the *Intifada* and the Israeli strategies for suppressing it are mild in comparison.

Of course, *any* discussion that involves Israel is conducted with the ghosts of millions of pogrom victims across the ages and six million European Jews murdered during the Holocaust. Add to all this the virulent hatred of Israel by Arab nations in recent times and the violence of many Islamic extremists in attacking Israelis. Remembering all this is important in interpreting the situation of Palestinian children in the *Intifada*.

The point is not to dismiss the harm done to the children by an appeal to some relative scale of awfulness ("What we do now is not as bad as what they did then"), or to whitewash the occupying forces. "To make an omelet you have to break some eggs," said an Israeli military official in rationalizing the casualties that resulted from attacking civilian population centers during the 1982 invasion of Lebanon. That's a despicable way to attempt to assuage consciences in the wake of acts resulting in children being killed, injured, and orphaned. It's as despicable coming from a military official of a government's army as it is from a terrorist who causes the death of a school full of children "for the cause." The point of all this is to put what follows in perspective.

Collective Punishment; Individual Suffering

For a child, only parents are more important than home as a foundation for security and identity. To destroy a child's house is to attack something fundamental to the child's being. The experiences of America's homeless children testify to this truth.

Demolition or the sealing of houses as a collective punishment for security offenses has a long history in the Israeli approach to occupation. It is common now as a tactic for combating the *Intifada*. One consequence is that families are forced to break up and move in with other relatives or to seek shelter in tents.

We have spoken with the children of these doubly "homeless" families. We have walked with them over the rubble of what was once their home. That this home was a two-room hovel is not the point. The point is to be found in the picture of a little boy and his sister holding the teddy bears we brought them, standing there amidst the rubble, truly homeless. Why? They are homeless because the Israeli authorities decided to teach their parents or older brothers or sisters a lesson in applied politics. The result: children caught between a rock and a hard place.

How common is this fate? According to a Save the Children Foundation report—the most comprehensive and detailed study of the impact of the *Intifada* on children in the West Bank and Gaza Strip—during the first two years of the Uprising, more than 1,000 homes were demolished or sealed, displacing more than 10,000 Palestinians, nearly 5,000 of them children (Nixon 1990).

Is Medical Care Political?

One consequence of being in a state of war, even limited war, is the politicization of all institutions. In extreme cases, this may take the form of using food as a weapon. In Sudan, for example, attempts to starve the enemy are a basic part of the strategy for the government fighting a rebellion in the southern provinces.

In the limited war of the *Intifada,* health care has become a weapon. According to the Association of Israeli and Palestinian Physicians for Human Rights, an Israeli group, medical care has worsened considerably because the Israeli occupation authorities have impeded or withheld medical services as a means of imposing individual and collective punishment. The number of patients from the West Bank and Gaza Strip receiving treatment in Israeli hospitals has shrunk dramatically since the *Intifada* began. Especially serious is the situation of seriously ill children: the 2,000 to 2,500 hospital hours previously allotted to children from the Occupied Territories has been slashed, affecting 30 percent of the children needing medical care in Gaza, and 65 percent of the children in the West Bank (*Jerusalem Post,* 8 February 1989).

One frequently employed tactic for suppressing the *Intifada* has been the imposition of twenty-four-hour curfews, in which entire villages or camps are put under a kind of house arrest for a period that may extend for days or even weeks. At least 75 percent of all children living in the West Bank and Gaza Strip have experienced curfew. Imposed curfews have a significant effect on the well-being of children. A World Health Organization delegation found that malnutrition in children was proportional to the amount of curfews imposed because parents were prevented from getting formula for their infants or food for their children (Nixon, 2:209–10).

Such curfews make medical care difficult, if not impossible, to obtain. This has an effect on children that goes well beyond dealing with injuries directly related to the *Intifada* itself. The prevention and treatment of diseases has suffered because parents are not able to bring sick children to hospitals or clinics during curfew. Simple health problems such as common colds may develop into life-threatening secondary conditions if not treated, particularly in the dismal conditions present in unheated houses in the chill of the West Bank winter.

As we walked through the camps in winter we found many children without socks and few children without runny noses. Furthermore, while a curfew is in effect, it is difficult, if not impossible, to send in an ambulance or a medical team to treat medical emergencies.

Is Education Political?

In the first year of the Uprising, all 1,194 primary and secondary schools in the West Bank were closed for at least nine out of twelve months, affecting over 300,000 school-age children. In the Gaza Strip, it is estimated that between one-third and one-half of all school days were lost during this same period (DataBase Project on Palestinian Human Rights 1989).

Some schools have been taken over as temporary military posts for the Israeli army; others are used as detention centers for those arrested. Vandalism, including broken windows and damaged or destroyed desks, chairs, and laboratory equipment, in schools used by the Israeli military has been reported by groups monitoring human rights violations.

As noted before, Israeli authorities explained the school closings (including nursery schools) as a response to the schools' supposed status as "hotbeds of disorder." In one sense they are: in a nationalist uprising all institutions are mobilized on behalf of the cause. If preserving the occupation is the Israeli definition of order, then the schools are hotbeds of *dis*order because they reflect and amplify the process of Palestinian "consciousness building."

But the policy of closing schools has been expanded to include the prohibition of any educational activities. Soldiers have even entered private homes to interrupt informal lessons taught by parents (*Jerusalem Post*, 25 November 1988).

The Israeli military also informed schools that the distribution of workbooks to primary and secondary schoolchildren for home study was forbidden. Teachers are punished and subject to having their homes demolished for holding informal classes when the schools are closed.

Perhaps this is the point: education is suspect. It is inherently revolutionary. *And,* because Palestinian parents value it as a source of upward mobility, it is a bargaining chip for the Israeli authorities to use as part of a carrot-and-stick approach to managing the conflict.

Human rights advocates have argued that the long-term closing of schools by the authority responsible for maintaining education is without international precedent. Banning education is a violation of both local and international law, neither of which permits the collective closure of educational institutions for protracted periods of time. But "international law" is not a strong force in the Middle East most of the time.

Given all this, it is not surprising that schools are often not safe places for children. When the schools are open, children have sometimes been teargassed in their classrooms, harassed, and beaten by soldiers entering the schools in search of demonstrators. Teachers cannot protect their students from the soldiers, and they themselves are intimidated and arrested in front of their students. One of the mothers we talked to told us about how Shin Beth agents (the Israeli secret service), police, and border guards entered a school for toddlers and preschoolers and arrested four of the seven teachers, pulling them out of school in front of the children. No charges were pressed, and all four were released several hours later. Our informant reported that her son was so severely shaken by the event that he now is fearful of going to school.

Children have also been exposed to violence by Palestinians in their classrooms. In the Gaza Strip, three high school teachers suspected of being collaborators were killed in front of their students (*Chicago Tribune* 19 November 1990).

In addition to schools, charitable institutions and social service agencies have also been closed by the Israeli military authorities. In'ash al-Usra (the Society for the Preservation of the Family), the largest charitable society on the West Bank, was closed, directly and indirectly affecting over 34,000 people, including 1,300 orphaned children. Licenses have been revoked from other charitable societies and youth centers, and other social centers have also been closed (DataBase Project on Palestinian Human Rights 1989). Although the war is limited in its military features, it is often total in its political and cultural dimensions.

Violence

Aside from the "cultural" hardships associated with the *Intifada*, since the beginning of the Uprising, most Palestinian children—not just those living in refugee camps—have been exposed directly or indirectly to violence (i.e., violence beyond what is "normal" in a culture in which corporal punishment is common in families and in schools).

Some children are injured accidentally when they are caught up in the political conflict; others are injured in a more deliberate manner—as increasingly younger children participate directly in demonstrations and as rules regarding the use of dangerous force by the military are relaxed.

Are children who participate in the *Intifada legitimate* targets of military and police efforts to suppress the revolt? Some who accept the legitimacy of the occupation say the answer must be yes, and they hold Palestinian parents and political leaders responsible for the injuries inflicted upon children. But what are the limits one should expect when police and soldiers armed with guns respond to large groups of children and adolescents armed with rocks—even if you do acknowledge the legitimacy of the occupation?

It is easy *in the abstract* to say that life is sacred and a child merits special protection. But what about when you are on the receiving end of rocks that can hurt, cause physical injury, and possibly even kill? We have been on the receiving end of such rocks, and we know the fear and rage *we* felt. If this were all there were to it, we might be able to make moral sense of what has happened and what continues to happen to the children of the *Intifada*. But, according to the accumulating evidence, it isn't.

Tear gas, potentially lethal "rubber" and "plastic" bullets, and live ammunition are used on children in a way that suggests something more than soldiers and police engaging in self-protection (Bishop 1989). Sometimes it seems like soldiers and police are "out of control." Children have been thrown onto burning tires and run over by military cars (Rädda Barnen 1989). They have been taken to rooftops by soldiers who then threaten to throw them off if the children do not comply with the soldiers' orders. One five-year-old child we met had a knife held to his throat while soldiers threatened to kill him if his grandmother did not provide information. Months later he reenacted this experience in every picture he drew and in every opportunity we gave him for doll play.

Who Is a Victim?

The army is authorized to arrest and punish anyone twelve years old or older who is caught throwing stones (*New York Times* 1989). But younger children are often detained. A seven-year-old from Bethlehem was arrested when an inspection of the contents of his bookbag showed a Palestinian flag doodled on a box (DataBase Project on Palestinian Human Rights 1989). The Save the Children Foundation study has documented children as young as five years old being arrested (Nixon 1990). We have spoken with children who have been arrested, and we have seen others in an Israeli prison.

It is estimated that thousands of Palestinian children have been arrested and detained by Israeli authorities since the beginning of the Uprising (DataBase Project on Palestinian Human Rights 1989). This is contrary not only to international legal norms, but also to Israeli military law as well. What is even more appalling is the abuse these youths suffer during their arrest and detention. As one thirteen-year-old testified:

> The soldiers came into my house at 1:00 in the morning, asking for the shebab [youth]. They found me, handcuffed and blindfolded me, and then started hitting me on my arms, stomach, thighs, and neck with their gun butts and sticks. They took me to the beach; it was winter and very cold. They took off the blindfold and all my clothes and beat me again for about five hours. They poured cold water all over me. Then they took me to Ansar 2 for interrogation. . . . I asked for water, but was told that I could only have it after I had confessed. . . . I was handcuffed and blindfolded. . . . They made me stand outside in the rain from dawn until sunset. I stood there, crying. This went on for two days. The first day I was interrogated for five hours, and then two hours the next day. They tried different ways to make me confess: once they said that they would put me by a fan to cut me to pieces; another time they brought a big box with a detective inside, screaming, to frighten me. They put me in the coffin [small, narrow closet] for three hours. I pounded on the door and cried the whole time. (Data-Base Project on Palestinian Human Rights 1989)

We met many children who suffered because they were in the wrong place at the wrong time. Muhammad, an eleven-year-old boy from Nablus, was passing near a demonstration on his way home from school when soldiers began shooting at the demonstrators. He ran and hid behind a wall until he heard the gunfire stop. When he peeked around the wall to see what was happening, a rubber bullet hit him in his eye, blinding him.

Another ten-year-old boy from Shufat refugee camp was standing near his house when a large force of border guards arrived in the camp and clashed with residents. The soldiers threw tear gas canisters at the demonstrators. One exploded in the boy's face, blinding him in one eye. Is this an "accident"?

The cost in human life and suffering has been great. By December 1990, nearly nine hundred Palestinians had died from gunshot wounds from live ammunition and rubber bullets, exposure to tear gas in confined areas, and internal injuries caused by severe beatings. Hundreds more had been killed by other Palestinians. Some were being "punished" for being collaborators or spies for the Israelis. Some were killings not directly related to the *Intifada*—nonpolitical enemies sometimes use the political turmoil as a convenient excuse to settle "private" scores. In a relatively small population these are significant numbers, even if they are not in the same league as Cambodia's millions killed or Mozambique's hundreds of thousands.

While the overwhelming majority of injuries and deaths associated with the *Intifada* through 1990 had been inflicted on Palestinians, 70 Israelis had also been killed (many in a single incident in which a Palestinian forced a bus off the road), and more than 1,000 Israeli civilians and 1,600 soldiers have been injured.

In 1990, the nature and ferocity of these attacks seemed to escalate in response to the killing of seventeen Palestinians by police at the Temple Mount/Haram al-Sharif in Jerusalem as part of a large conflict between Israeli border guards and Muslim worshipers. Islamic fundamentalist extremists called for violent revenge. A number of Israelis were stabbed in the weeks that followed—sometimes as a matter of policy, sometimes as sorrowful Palestinians tried to take personal revenge. In many ways the events of 1990 strengthened the hands of extremists on both sides and undercut the efforts of "moderates" inclined to seek some sort of political compromise.

Israeli casualties have included children wounded or killed. This is not a one-sided massacre. This is limited war. Both sides suffer casualties. But the numbers reflect the weapons and tactics available to each side: Palestinians, armed mainly with rocks, have suffered far more injuries and deaths than the Israelis, who have guns, tanks, and a wide array of weaponry.

The *Intifada* dead as of December 1989 included 159 children aged sixteen and younger. The average age of children killed was ten. It is estimated that between 50,000 and 63,000 children were seriously injured during the first two years of the *Intifada* (i.e., at least one out of every twenty children required medical treatment for their injuries) (Nixon 1990, 1:xv). Taking into consideration the relative differences between Palestinian and American population sizes, such losses would be equivalent to more than 9,000 American children killed and more than 3 million seriously injured.

One of the most disturbing conclusions of the Save the Children report and other investigations by human rights groups is that the shooting of children does not appear to be random (Nixon 1990, 1:xv). Save the Children investigators prepared meticulous accounts of each child's death. Their conclusions are sobering. Looking over the course of the first two years of the *Intifada,* they found that Palestinian children were increasingly becoming the targets of live ammunition. In the beginning of the Uprising, Israeli soldiers tended to fire randomly and usually did not hit vital organs. As the *Intifada* "progressed," the confrontations between soldiers and civilians tended to become much smaller, and were often provoked by soldiers entering villages or refugee camps to make arrests or carry out house-to-house searches (Bishop 1989). Of the 159 child deaths in the first two years of the *Intifada,* gunfire was the leading cause of death, accounting for 67 percent of all child deaths. All of the children killed by gunfire were hit directly except for one child killed by a ricocheting bullet. Some 48 percent of the children killed by gunfire had been shot in the head or neck, while nearly one-fifth of the children suffered multiple gunshot wounds. Twelve percent of the children were shot from behind. The majority of children who were shot but did not die had also been shot in the upper body, including the head, or had suffered multiple gunshot wounds (Nixon 1990, 1:xvi).

Rubber Bullets, Broken Children

The use of "rubber" and "plastic" bullets has increased. Approximately 6,500 to 8,500 children were injured by gunfire during the first two years of the Uprising. Rubber bullets are round marble-sized metal balls covered with a thin coating of black hard rubber. In appearance, the new marble bullet introduced in December 1988 looks much like the "aggie" children use as the target in the game of marbles. Weighing twenty grams, its effect is far from child's play. The plastic bullets, composed of glass and metal and covered with an extremely hard coating of plastic, can be lethal when used at a range closer than seventy meters.

According to reports, these bullets have caused severe injuries to a number of children, including serious damage to internal organs, blindness, and brain damage. Some injuries have been fatal (Kifner,

14 January 1989). In September 1988 Defense Minister Yitzak Rabin gave approval for the use of plastic bullets, saying, "Our purpose is to increase the number of wounded among those who take part in violent activities, but not to kill them. . . . The rioters are suffering more casualties. That is precisely our aim" (*Financial Times*, 29 September 1988). At least 170 children were shot in the first five weeks after this new policy was announced (DataBase Project on Palestinian Human Rights 1989).

In January 1989 Rabin sanctioned the shooting of demonstrators trying to escape. Furthermore, noncommissioned officers were authorized to open fire with plastic ammunition at stone-throwing demonstrators (Rädda Barnen 1989). More recently, orders have been given to fire at masked youths.

Tear Gas: Made in the U.S.A.

It has been estimated that more than 10,000 children required medical treatment for tear gas–related injuries during the first two years of the *Intifada* (Nixon 1990). Children have also been killed by tear gas: during the first eleven months of the Uprising, 31 children died after exposure to it. Tear gas grenades have been thrown into houses, narrow streets, classrooms, hospitals, and maternity wards, although it is against regulations to use it in enclosed spaces. In 84 percent of the cases investigated, "a tear gas canister was launched into the house or within five meters of an open door or window of the house" (Nixon 1990, 1:xiii–xiv).

Doctors working in the Occupied Territories have noted recurrent breathing difficulties, abdominal pains, severe vomiting, and unconsciousness when treating people exposed to tear gas. Small children are particularly vulnerable to severe medical problems. Furthermore, there have been frequent reports of increased risk of miscarriages among women who have been teargassed during pregnancy. In the camps in the Gaza Strip, which come under frequent tear gas attacks, the rate of miscarriages has increased fourfold from what it was before the *Intifada*, according to health professionals in the area.

Early in the *Intifada* it was common for Palestinians to present visiting Americans with spent tear gas canisters, plainly marked "Made in the U.S.A." They would say, "I am returning this to you so you can take it back with you to the United States where it belongs. Why do you send us such presents?"

The U.S. manufacturer, Federal Laboratories, has announced that their tear gas is only intended for use in the open air to quell riots and under no circumstances should be used in enclosed areas. Federal Laboratories officially suspended their sales of tear gas to Israel in May 1988 in response to evidence of deliberate Israeli misuse of their product. But according to reports from the field, these tear gas canisters were still in use at the end of the year—with the date of production and the manufacturer's name no longer printed on the canister. Furthermore, the vice president of the parent company of Federal Laboratories, TransTechnology Corporation, stated that "the State Department has approved shipments of tear gas to Israel, and we support that stand" (Nixon 1990).

Child Abuse as Public Policy?

If an American parent beat a child so severely that the child's arm broke, we would be quick to label his or her action child abuse. If an Israeli or Palestinian parent did the same to a child in his or her care, the same label would apply. If an American policeman beat a delinquent youth so badly that the youth required hospital attention, no doubt a charge of "police brutality" would be filed. If that beating was administered by a staff person in a juvenile detention facility, "institutional child abuse" would be charged. The same would be true in Israel. But does the concept of child abuse apply in a situation of "limited war"?

What do we call it when more than 25,000 children required medical treatment for beating injuries during the first two years of the *Intifada* (Nixon 1990, 1:xvi)? Many of these children were active participants in the *Intifada*—throwing rocks, displaying outlawed flags, singing prohibited songs, harassing soldiers and police. Some would say that such behavior justifies the use of damaging force.

Of the injured children and youth, approximately 7,000 children were age ten and under and 4,000 were age five and under. Over 80 percent of the children requiring treatment had been beaten on their heads and upper bodies and at multiple locations (Nixon 1990, 1:xvi). Do the same standards apply to Israelis responding to the

Intifada as apply to parents, police, and counselors dealing with "unruly" kids in Israel and the United States? Or do we apply the standards of Iraq and Syria and Saudi Arabia?

In reviewing Uprising-related cases, a delegation from Physicians for Human Rights found that the pattern of beating injuries "suggests a deliberate policy . . . designed to disable and not to kill, to inflict maximum damage while reducing the risk of death. Cases of fractured arms were frequent (the person's arm is forcibly extended until the radius is broken in midshaft) as well as fractures on the hands. It seemed more a planned and purposeful form of brutalization, indiscriminate in choice of victim but precise in the choice of injury" (Physicians for Human Rights 1988).

Official statements condone the violent behavior of soldiers. In January 1988 Rabin announced his "Iron Fist policy" of "force, power, and blows" to prevent demonstrations. In the weeks following, the number of children requiring medical treatment for injuries from beatings rose dramatically. Soldiers attacked demonstrators, including youth, with wooden sticks, truncheons, and rifle butts (Greenberg, 1988).

The United Nations Relief and Works Agency (UNWRA) reports that in the Gaza Strip, 58 percent of those treated for injuries during the first year of the Uprising were children under fifteen. Some 30 percent of West Bank injuries involved children sixteen and younger (DataBase Project on Palestinian Human Rights 1989). What standards should we apply to evaluating those who inflicted these injuries?

Child Neglect?

Who is responsible when children are injured in "preventable accidents"? Here the controversy is very hot indeed. Are Palestinians to blame for putting their children "in harm's way" by virtue of continuing the *Intifada* rather than backing down and accepting "peace" on Israeli terms? Are Palestinian parents neglectful for allowing their children to participate in demonstrations and violent conflicts with soldiers?

Some Israelis argue that the answer must be a resounding "yes." "What kind of parents would subject their children to such risks?" they ask. Others argue that Palestinian political leaders are callously using children as human shields to protect adult demonstrators. Or they say that Palestinian adults are cynically or fanatically offering up children as cannon fodder, as "martyrs" who can be used to exploit media attention and manipulate the emotions of susceptible Americans and Europeans. Do Palestinian parents "love" their children? How do we assess responsibility when many parents often feel they have little ability to control what their children do, and certainly have difficulty telling them to hang back from the confrontations and risk being called cowards and traitors by their peers?

The UN Convention on the Rights of the Child prohibits nations from using children aged fifteen or younger as soldiers. Are Palestinians violating the spirit and letter of the UN convention by employing children as "soldiers"? Is the "collective neglect" to be laid at the doorstep of the Palestinians? The Israeli Ministry of Justice in 1989 issued a statement making that claim.

Like most everything in the Israeli-Palestinian conflict, the issue of collective child neglect is a mosaic of shared responsibilities and disputed realities. For example, children have been injured when incendiary objects have been dropped from helicopters as part of Israeli military operations. These objects, used to light up military targets, produce flames when they come in contact with children's bodies, causing second- and third-degree burns on their faces, arms, legs, and abdomens. Three children were killed by these exploding devices. It has been proven that these military operations were carried out over populated areas and not over firing ranges (Nixon 1990, 2:349–350). The flares that malfunction and fall to the ground cause severe burns to children who step on them or pick them up. These "incendiary sticks" are believed to be made in the U.S. Who is responsible for these injuries?

Children do participate in direct confrontations with the military, of course. Preadolescent rock throwers are common, and many children are quick to flash the prohibited "V" (victory) sign and to sing outlawed patriotic songs. By most accounts, this direct participation is growing, in part because of depletion of the ranks of adolescents and young adults.

This shift was evident in early 1989, as the average age of the wounded and killed decreased. Children accounted for 21 percent of all recorded deaths and 38 percent of all recorded casualties (deaths and injuries).

When children were injured while participating in, or just being in the vicinity of, a demonstration, medical assistance was often obstructed or delayed by direct military interference, shooting, or curfew. In over 80 percent of the cases of children mortally wounded by gunfire and who sought treatment, access to medical care was obstructed or delayed by the army. In almost 20 percent of these cases, the wounded child was taken into detention and died in military custody (Nixon 1990, 2:145).

Children have been attacked or arrested in ambulances, in clinics, in hospitals, and even while being operated on. Many clinics and hospitals in the Occupied Territories have experienced tear gas attacks and shooting on the premises. Staff have been shot, beaten, and exposed to tear gas while executing their professional duties (World Health Organization 1989).

Israeli soldiers have prevented Red Crescent ambulances from evacuating the injured. One eyewitness account describes an eleven-year-old child shot by soldiers and left bleeding on the main street for six hours, while medical teams were prevented by the army from helping him. When the child was finally taken to the hospital, he died from loss of blood (World Health Organization 1989).

The supervisor of the Nablus Red Crescent reported that not only are ambulances regularly denied access to scenes of violence, but that the ambulances are often hijacked by the soldiers who beat the drivers and nurses. We have seen this firsthand. On our way to visit a young girl in a hospital who had been shot the day before by soldiers, we saw a Red Crescent ambulance transferring a boy who had just been shot by soldiers earlier that morning to another hospital. The boy, of course, was bandaged, but the ambulance driver's head was also bandaged and bloody. The driver had been clubbed by the soldiers as he tried to help the boy into the ambulance.

Earlier that day at the same hospital, soldiers had burst into the operating room, looking for people they had shot so they could arrest them. Who is responsible? Is it those who rebel or those who seek to suppress that rebellion? It's easy for those inside the conflict to point fingers at the other side; it's easy for the outsider to blame both sides. But does placing blame solve the problem for the children?

Places of Safety and Places of Danger

Conflict and stress are linked for children and families trapped in the political conflict in the West Bank and Gaza. Places where children have traditionally been safe—home and school—no longer offer security in many cases. Half the children killed were not in the vicinity of a protest activity when killed. Some 40 percent of all children who died were at home or within ten meters of their home when they were killed (Nixon 1990, 1:xv).

In addition to the acute, traumatic, and dramatically destructive cases (such as forcing a family to remain inside a house after tear gas had been thrown in through the window) that harm children, chronic, low-grade threats undermine day-to-day life for children.

The military curfews imposed in many areas have presented special problems for young children. For example, in the worst-hit refugee camps, toddlers have been confined to their two-room houses for many days on end and prohibited from going outside to play, producing a great deal of strain between parents and children. Who is responsible? Why not just surrender to the occupation? Why not just withdraw from the conflict?

What does it mean when Palestinian parents tell us that they feel unable to protect their children from these dangers? Palestinians often speak of "steadfastness" as a virtue. Does this steadfast commitment to the cause of regaining their homeland make them responsible for the injuries sustained by their children? Who is responsible for children being caught between a rock and a hard place?

It is common, especially in refugee camps and in the towns and cities where demonstrations occur, for soldiers to raid homes and carry out searches looking for information about demonstrators. Often these raids occur at night. Often intimidation, threats, and force are used to extract information. Parents have reported that their homes have been entered repeatedly, sometimes more than once per night for extended periods. What could be more important than protecting their children from all this?

Some Palestinians have chosen to leave the situation—perhaps to go to the United States or to Europe. Emigration rates have increased since the *Intifada* began (and once Palestinians leave they may never receive permission to return). Those who stay and seek to stay out of the struggle are called "Kitkats." The word connotes "wimp" and "effete" and "coward."

We sat one day in Ramallah with a family in which the fourteen-year-old was being held back from participating in the conflict by his parents. His older brother was already in prison. The parents were awaiting permission to emigrate—and had been told that they could take their imprisoned son with them if they agree to leave permanently. The boy was sheepish, even ashamed. He knew what it means to be a Kitkat. What price physical safety?

Consequences of Growing Up in the *Intifada*

The beatings, the shootings, the teargassings, the curfews have taken their toll on this young population, particularly among the youngest children. A recent study has found increased behavioral and psychological symptoms for Palestinian children exposed to military violence (Baker 1989). Teachers and parents have also reported increases in fearfulness, aggression, anxiety, bed-wetting, and depression among the children of the West Bank and Gaza. They have nightmares and other sleep-related disorders.

We met a toddler who had been shot in the face. Her mother had carried her to an outside balcony to look below at a confrontation between soldiers and villagers. The soldiers shot up at the gathering crowd on the balcony. The little girl was shot while in the arms of her mother. She is now blind in one eye, and her face is partially paralyzed. Her mother told us that she had been a quiet and calm child before the shooting. Since then, her mother reports that she is very nervous. She hides in the house every time she hears shooting or a commotion outside, saying, "They'll shoot" and pointing to her eye. Since the event, soldiers have repeatedly come back to the house. The child hides and physically shakes.

A four-year-old witnessed the beating of his older brother. Soldiers beat the brother and kicked him. Two days later, in another attack, the brother was killed by the soldiers. The four-year-old broke out in a rash that completely covered his body. He was hospitalized for seven days.

Drawings by Palestinian children reflect the violence of their daily lives. Pictures of where they live depict children being grabbed, beaten, or shot by soldiers in the context of going to school, staying at home, or participating in demonstrations. One drawing shows a house literally bursting with the stresses of living with the *Intifada* — stress lines radiate from the house in all directions.

However, Palestinian children are also imbued with nationalism. In addition to violence, their drawings almost invariably feature Palestinian flags, often in ingenious ways, for example, the flag as the window of a house, the flag worked into clothing, the flag carried in the beak of a bird. A few children simply drew pictures of the Palestinian flag covering the entire paper in response to being asked to draw where they live.

Numerous observers have suggested that ideology helps parents cope with the stresses and fears of living in a war zone or living under oppressive conditions. Bettelheim (1943) reported that those who did best in the Nazi concentration camps were the ultra-religious and the Communists because members of both groups had a transcendent belief system that could not be touched by day-to-day horror and deprivation. Punamaki has reported that nationalist ideology serves the same function for Palestinian parents: it supports them so they can support their children (Punamaki 1987). Studies in World War II found that the best predictor of children's response to living with the daily bombing of their homeland was their parents' ability to cope (Janis 1951). All this puts us in a bind: powerful ideology supports parents psychologically and thus serves as a resource for children under stress. But this same ideology may fuel the conflict that causes the stress and may inhibit compromise solutions. Children are caught between a rock and a hard place.

The End of the Line

Mansur, age nine, had been wounded when a grenade exploded in the family's yard when they were having dinner. Who was responsible for this explosion? There is no documentation that clarifies this issue, so we can focus on the experience of the children.

Mansur's whole family—eight brothers and sisters and his mother and father—had also been injured. When we entered his hospital room, Mansur was in a wheelchair, wheeling around the room at a dizzying pace. He operated the wheelchair with one arm because the other had been blown off. He had no legs because they had also been blown off by the grenade. Also as a result of the explosion, he was completely blind in one eye and 60 percent blind in the other.

His sister, Sabah, age fourteen, was also in the hospital as a result of the grenade. She was also in a wheelchair, having sustained fractures in her legs from the explosion. She had been channeling her energy into artistic pursuits. A talented young artist, she showed us drawing after drawing that she had made during her two months in the hospital. Some were of soldiers shooting and beating children. Others were of Palestinians demonstrating against the soldiers or raising the Palestinian flag. They expressed the suffering, the struggle, the violence, and also the hope of an oppressed people. She gave us two of her drawings to take with us. One was of a young boy's face—sad, but serious. A Palestinian flag flew where his body should have been. Her brother perhaps? The other showed the face of an older boy with a gun at his side. Only his fierce eyes were visible behind his *kufiya*. The Palestinian flag hung in the background. Or was this her brother a few years from now? Would Mansur have a homeland while he was still a child, or would this one-armed boy "take up arms" in the years to come?

In January 1990 a group of Israelis and Palestinians seeking peace, justice, and reconciliation were joined by a crowd of international sympathizers in a demonstration in Jerusalem. They formed a chain around the old city. Near the Damascus Gate many people were chanting "We want peace." Some were chanting nationalistic slogans. The government forces present turned on water cannons, and powerful jets of water sprayed dye on the crowd (dye so that when the soldiers and police went looking for participants later they could identify them). And with the water came tear gas and rubber bullets. People were running. A small boy had fallen and was getting trampled underfoot. We helped him up. An Italian woman inside a hotel was blinded in one eye when a torrent of water from a water cannon shattered the window through which she was watching the demonstration.

Shortly after this we met a young girl of about ten and her small sister. She wanted to know where the march was. We said we didn't think there was going to be one. She told us that the police had taken her and her sister in the police car to the police station where they had been held for several hours. Her little sister still looked terrified. We asked her if she was afraid. She said that she was, but that she wanted to go to the march because it was important for her to be there. Who is responsible for this little girl and her sister? Who?

7

Chicago:

The War Close to Home

About two months before I had my baby, I was just walking, going to my sister's house. And the boys [gang members] came running, shooting. They were shooting at each other. And it was frightening, too. Because, I had my little girl [a three-year-old], and I didn't know which way to run. We just laid on the ground until they got through. I laid on top of her. There were about four or five shots. But it was just the idea that we had to get down on the ground. She was screaming, and I was trying to calm her down. After, we didn't go outside that day. We just went back upstairs. That's all.

  —Shirley, twenty-one, Cabrini Green, Chicago, 1990

Shirley and her children live in a high-rise public housing development in the United States. A comparison of her gang-controlled neighborhood to a war zone serves to underscore the heightened physical danger that Shirley and other poor Americans living in urban areas must face. Officially, war is defined as a conflict in which at least one thousand people die (Sivard 1989, 23). According to the U.S. Federal Bureau of Investigation (cited in Zinsmeister 1990), two thousand minors were murdered in the United States in 1988. This figure is 50 percent higher than the figure in 1985.

In recent years the major urban centers of the United States have experienced a dramatic growth of youth gangs. These gangs war with each other and with mainstream society. Fueled by the underground drug economy and the breakdown of traditional institutions of social control, gangs have contributed to a rapid increase in the numbers of homicides, aggravated assaults, rapes, and other kinds of interpersonal violence committed in the United States (Seever 1990).

Between 1960 and 1980 the homicide rate in the United States doubled. Murders in New York City, Chicago, Los Angeles, Detroit, and Philadelphia accounted for a significant percent of this increase (Chilton 1987, 195). Bystander shootings more than tripled in New York, Los Angeles, Washington, and Boston between 1985 and 1988 (Gross 1990, 14). For black males and females aged fifteen to thirty-four, homicide is the leading cause of death (Secretary's Task Force on Black and Minority Health 1985, 160).

But even these terrible figures hide a worse truth. Medical technology has improved so much in the last twenty years that many of those who are now wounded in incidents of violence would have died had they experienced the same injuries in the 1970s. This is important to remember as we note that the rate of serious assault has increased by 400 percent in American cities like Chicago when we compare the rates in the mid-1970s with the rate in 1990.

The escalating level of violence associated with drugs, gangs, and organized crime is a growing concern for American society. Whole communities are being described as war zones, where gangs use fear to control the daily lives of residents. For example, a gang in Chicago imposed an early evening curfew on an entire public housing building population by threatening to shoot violators (Caseso and Blau 1989, 16).

Although gangs are not a new phenomenon on the urban scene, most observers note that they are fundamentally different today. More of them exist in more communities. Gangs have increased adult involvement, are more organized, and are active in more illegal enterprises (Seever 1990).

Public Housing or Internal Refugee Camps?

Taylor Homes is the largest public housing development in Chicago. The twenty-eight sixteen-story buildings sit on ninety-two acres and house approximately 20,000 people. In one sense, Taylor Homes is the site of a massive camp for America's internal refugees, the families who are displaced from "regular" communities in the city.

In the first quarter of 1988, twenty-six major crimes were reported compared to 441 in the first three months of 1989. The district police commander for Taylor estimates that "more than two thirds of the crimes committed are related to rapidly expanding narcotics sales" (Caseso and Blau 1989, 16).

In 1989 the police district serving another Chicago public housing development recorded 318 aggravated assaults. Twenty-two percent of the assaults were committed with a gun, 28 percent with knives, and 48 percent with "other dangerous weapons." Gang weaponry is increasingly sophisticated (Seever 1990). For example, a police raid on one apartment building in a crime-ridden community in Chicago yielded "five handguns, three rifles, two shotguns, two pounds of plastic explosives, blasting caps, [and] a vast assortment of ammunition" (*Chicago Sun Times*, 10 August 1989). In the first six months of 1990 Chicago police seized 8,289 weapons (Blau 1990, 1). According to the state's attorney's office, "Thirty years ago, gangs had zip guns—single-shot, homemade, primitive. Now these gang-bangers have 'sprayers' and automatic weapons that simulate the weapons of armies" (Blau 1990, 1).

Many of the guns are purchased legally outside city limits and sold in Chicago illegally. In one extreme case, arms negotiations between a local gang and a foreign country were reported. A leader of a Chicago gang and Muammar Qaddafi of Libya were stopped from implementing planned terrorist activities in the United States, which included the sale of rocket launchers to the gang leader. Gangs maintain powerful images in the community, and threaten police and other law enforcement officials who would otherwise provide protection to families.

There are 64 million children in America. Of these, 48 million live in urban communities, and one-fifth of these children, almost 13 million, are living in poverty (Zinsmeister 1990). Media confront us regularly with reports of "Growing Up Scared" (Zinsmeister 1990), "Can the Children Be Saved?" (Morganthau 1989), and "Child in Wrong Place at Wrong Time Is Blinded" (Blau 6 April 1990). These reports underscore the pervasiveness of the problem and point to some urban environments as particularly dangerous.

In the United States public housing developments are home to approximately 1.6 million children (National Association of Housing Redevelopment Officials 1989). These developments include some of the highest crime communities in the country. For example, in 1980, 11 percent of the murders in Chicago, 9 percent of the rapes, and 10 percent of the aggravated assaults were committed in the Robert Taylor Homes development (Sheppard 1980). Additionally, public housing represents some of the most impoverished communities in the country. Recognizing the depressed state of housing under their authority, the federal government has recently established a National Commission on Stressed Public Housing to recommend reforms.

Poor Children, Poor Prospects

Economic deprivation is generally recognized as the principal source of sociocultural risk to children. In America, half of the poor people are children (Edelman 1987). The federal government sets the official poverty line based on income. The amount is set to reflect the minimum dollars needed by a family to meet basic living needs. In 1984 the poverty line for a family of four was $10,609. However, 42 percent of poor families lived below 50 percent of the poverty line in 1983 (Edelman 1987, 26). For example, the median annual income of families living in all Chicago public housing developments was just $4,650 (Chicago Housing Authority 1985, 75).

Black children have a one in two chance of being poor. If they are born to a single mother, their chances of being poor are two out of three. For the same child born to a poor mother under twenty-five, the chances of being poor increase to a staggering four out of five (Edelman 1987, 3).

Low national reading scores and drop-out rates among children who attend Chicago's inner-city public school system have drawn considerable media attention. In 1980, 39,500 children were enrolled in Chicago's segregated inner-city ninth-grade classrooms. Four years later only 47 percent graduated, and of those, only one-third of the students tested above the national average twelfth-grade reading level (Wilson 1987, 57). The cause of school failure, the failure of teachers to teach effectively, and the failure of children to learn is a complex issue. However, recent research identifies chronic stress as one of the most significant risk factors.

For example, experiencing physical illness in the family, the death of a family member, or a parent's job loss were events that influenced children's intelligence scores (Sameroff 1987). Additionally, changes in children's behavior in reaction to stress can negatively affect their school performance (Gardner 1971). A child who becomes withdrawn or aggressive toward his classmates cannot fully participate in the social learning environment of school.

Out of the Mainstream, into the Firing Line

We observed Chicago's public housing developments at close range to understand an environment that is isolated from mainstream society. Though many of the housing developments exist side by side with more affluent communities, the line between them is rarely crossed. The perception of danger in the projects is a factor in this separation, but race also has an impact according to a report by the Illinois Criminal Justice Information Authority. Their studies "found Chicago to be the most racially segregated major city in the United States. In the course of a day, there is only a 1 in 25 chance that a black in Chicago will see a white in his neighborhood or that a white will see a black in his community" (1986).

Absence of attention to the physical plant of the public housing neighborhood is immediately evident. Buildings and grounds are in constant disrepair. The drive into one public housing parking lot in Chicago is full of potholes. The craters are large enough to swallow an automobile tire, and each spring they become deeper and wider. The parking lot is almost empty. A few older-model-cars are parked along the periphery. The high-rise buildings stand amidst vacant lots and playgrounds devoid of plantings and functional equipment. One rarely sees children playing outside.

Sniping incidents have prompted housing residents to nickname the tall buildings "gun towers." The walls of the buildings are covered with graffiti, and the open staircase hallways are dark and dank. Vandalism has transformed a wall of mailboxes located in the common breezeway connecting the buildings into a twisted mass of metal with open holes. Many windows in the ten-story buildings are boarded up.

Funding for community health and mental health facilities and programs has been tenuous over the past years, and recently entire facilities have been closed. Access to alternative health care services requires extensive travel.

There are no on-site laundry facilities for the more than six thousand residents of this housing complex. The closest laundromat is one mile away. Additionally, no supermarket and no library are within walking distance. The local grocery store preys on the captive resident population, selling low-quality merchandise at high prices. Small businesses have moved out of the neighborhood, taking services and job opportunities away from the community. Importing services is extremely difficult because providers from outside the community are afraid to come in.

Cab drivers and delivery men have been robbed in the course of picking up passengers and delivering goods. Several companies canceled laundry service and milk delivery to a day care center located in public housing after individual drivers were robbed and assaulted. Additionally, human service providers such as teachers, visiting health workers, and emergency workers often face great risk when performing their jobs in this dangerous environment. The extreme isolation characteristic of life in a place like Taylor Homes complicates the risks of being poor in America.

Gandhi once said that poverty was the worst form of violence. Experienced in an atmosphere of extreme danger, poverty cuts deeply into the fabric of family life and has profound implications for children's development. Young children do not ordinarily participate in criminal activity directly. However, their presence in the environment increases their risk of physical and psychological harm. For example, in Chicago, over 100,000 children live in public housing (Chicago Housing Authority 1985). A recent analysis of Chicago's police data (Reardon 1988) revealed that the officially reported rate of violent crime victimization for residents of housing developments was 50 percent higher than for the city as a whole (34 per 1,000 vs. 23 per 1,000). This means that children in public housing projects are twice as likely as other children to be exposed to violent crime (since the overall 23 per 1,000 victimization rate includes the housing projects, which inflates the overall figure substantially). Similarly, the New York City Departments of Planning and Health report the homicide rate in the Harlem community at 71.3 per 100,000 people in contrast to a rate of 27.5 per 100,000 for New York City as a whole (Terry 1990).

In a national study conducted by the Department of Housing and Urban Development, crime committed in public housing was compared with crime in the host city. The report indicated that property crime was slightly lower and personal crime higher in public housing than in the city as a whole (National Association of Housing Redevelopment Officials 1989).

Children Exposed to Violent Crime

The rate at which children are exposed to violent crime in these neighborhoods is alarming. A visitor to a Washington, D.C., eighth-grade classroom asked the nineteen thirteen-year-olds, "How many of you know somebody who's been killed?" Fourteen hands went up. When the children were asked how the killings had happened, they responded, "shot, stabbed, shot, shot, drugs, shot" (Zinsmeister 1990). A survey conducted by Chicago's Community Mental Health Council found that nearly 40 percent of one thousand Chicago high school and elementary school students had witnessed a shooting, more than 33 percent had seen a stabbing, and 25 percent had seen a murder (Kotulak 1990, 1).

In Baltimore 168 teens, seeking routine medical services at an inner-city health clinic, were screened for exposure to violence. The teens indicated that they had been the victim of violence an average of one and a half times each. Twenty percent of the teens reported that their experiences constituted a serious threat to their lives (Zinsmeister 1990).

Los Angeles County law enforcement officials estimate that 10 to 20 percent of the annual two thousand homicides are witnessed by dependent children (Pynoos and Eth 1986). Additionally, research focused on the routine occurrence and effects of exposure to environmental violence for children living in public housing in Chicago revealed that every child in the sample had firsthand encounters with shooting by age five (Dubrow and Garbarino 1989).

Child Victims of Crime in Chicago

Urica was only six years old when two men, high on cocaine, broke into her family's apartment seeking drug money. In the struggle that ensued, she witnessed the murder of her mother and her younger sister. Urica was stabbed forty-eight times and left for dead by the assailants. But Urica was "playing dead," a performance that saved her life. Her thirteen-year-old cousin discovered the scene the following morning and reported it to relatives. Urica and an infant sister survived the attack. Her physical recovery was a miracle by medical standards, but the psychological trauma is lasting. Urica found some justice in the courtroom when she was able to identify the two men who killed her family. They were convicted, and a jury imposed the death sentence. Today, Urica continues to receive professional counseling to help her cope with the consequences of the event.

Nine-year-old Alonzo was walking through his public housing complex when he was shot in the head. The bullet was intended for a neighborhood teen, according to reports, but it hit Alonzo. He recovered completely from his physical injuries, but he was left emotionally scarred by this experience. Alonzo told a reporter after the incident, "I don't want to go back there and live" (Thornton 1988). Like many of the children we talked with in public housing environments, he wants to live where it is safe.

A newspaper article called Robert the "child in the wrong place at the wrong time" (Blau 6 April 1990). Robert is ten. He was hit by a bullet on his way home from a friend's house. The bullet, shot in a drug-related gang rivalry, entered one side of his skull and came out on the other side. Robert is blind. How will he survive the terror of not being able to see?

We visited three afterschool programs serving high-crime inner-city neighborhoods in Chicago. The programs are funded by the Illinois Department of Children and Family Services (IDCFS) and operated by private social service agencies (Chicago Commons Association, the Salvation Army, and Lutheran Social Services). Children between the ages of six and twelve participate in educational and recreational activities each afternoon at the centers. The programs support community parents who are enrolled full-time in educational programs or working full-time.

An eleven-year-old child who lives in a high-rise public housing development in Chicago described her experience with exposure to gunfire. She walks from the local elementary school through the development to reach a community-based afterschool program. One day, she was between school and the center when shooting started. She heard someone yell, "They're shooting, get down," and she immediately dropped to the ground and proceeded to crawl on her hands and knees to the center. She said, "I was really scared."

On the near north side of the city, staff reported that a child arrived at their center, saying that she observed two men killing another man and stuffing the body into a garbage can. The director called the police, who investigated and confirmed the child's information. The police found a man who had been severely beaten.

We asked children to draw pictures of where they live to further understand their experiences in the environment. During one drawing session a twelve-year-old girl told us: "Once I was in the car, waiting outside my house with my auntie and my cousins. I was in the backseat. I saw some Disciples [a Chicago gang] with Uzies [automatic guns]. I got so scared. I got down on the floor of the car." A seven-year-old boy drew a picture of "two gang-bangers, one with a bottle and one with a bat." There was a police car in the picture, and the policeman was in the process of arresting and handcuffing the gang members. We asked him if he had ever seen people arrested. He responded, "Yes, lots of times."

Children's Reactions to Violence

Stressful life events affect children's learning and psychological well-being. Young children have little control over the environmental danger that surrounds them in an inner-city neighborhood. To survive, however, they cope. Some children attempt to forget experiences with violent events, and other children reexperience the events in play activities or by drawing pictures of what happened. Additionally, teachers and parents observe changes in children's behavior and in children's ability to learn.

Relatives note that Urica began to suck her thumb after her family was murdered. According to teachers, her school grades now fluctuate, and she is aggressive toward other children in the classroom. Urica says that she is not afraid of danger. Alonzo's mother reports that since he was shot, he bites his nails and stutters. He has trouble concentrating, he is forgetful, and he has difficulty learning in school (Marin 1989).

A social worker with the Chicago public schools found that exposure to violence had a significant impact on learning and behavior problems in school. In her studies of six children with learning and behavior problems from one classroom on the south side of Chicago, she found that all these children had experienced the murder of a close family member. Their experiences not only affected their individual ability to function in the classroom, but their collective behavior was disruptive to the entire classroom (Dyson 1989).

We interviewed preschool teachers in Head Start and day care programs in Chicago. They reported the impact of exposure to chronic violence on children's development. Teachers regularly observe children as young as three years old playing at shooting up drugs, strutting like "gang-bangers," and taking turns being victims, mourners, and preachers as they act out the common occurrence of funerals resulting from gang warfare. Children's artwork contains gang symbols and events such as shootings, stabbings, and arrests.

A preschool teacher reported that she instructed all of the three- and four-year-old children to get down on the floor one day when shooting started outside the classroom window. The teachers said that one little girl has not been the same since the incident. The girl physically shakes and expresses concern that something will happen to her mother while she is at school.

Unfortunately, for three sisters aged eight, ten, and twelve, this fear became a reality. Their mother was shot in the throat while walking with a relative down a commercial avenue in mid-afternoon. One gang member exchanged gunfire with another during a drive-by shooting, and the two women were "caught in the crossfire." Her condition was serious. She was rushed to a hospital and admitted to intensive care, requiring special assistance to breathe. She was unable to speak, and doctors did not know whether she would regain the use of her voice. When she was released from the hospital she had an open hole in her throat with a breathing tube protruding. The youngest daughter was observed in her afterschool program by the teacher. She reported that the girl complained that her throat hurt and said, "My throat itches." She began to scratch her neck in one place, developing a red mark on her neck. Additionally, the mother role played out in the classroom now included placement of a tissue or a piece of cloth over the mark on her neck.

Four months after the incident we asked two of the children to draw a picture of their family. One girl drew a picture of her dad bringing her mother home from the hospital after the incident. The mother figure had a bandage on her neck. The other child drew a picture titled "guy shooting my mom." She drew the drive-by vehicle with bullets coming out of the car window and hitting her mother.

Parents report significant behavioral changes in children exposed to urban violence. Regressive behavior, such as the loss of toilet training, was reported by mothers during the interviews. A mother reported that her five-year-old daughter began to wet the bed. She consulted her physician about the problem and was told that the bed-wetting might be a reaction to the child's new baby sister. However, the bed-wetting continued for two more years. One day the child confided in her mother that she was afraid to get up because of the shooting outside. She chose to stay in bed and wet herself out of fear.

Exaggerated startle reactions ("shell shock") have been observed by mothers. For example, in June 1989, one mother and her five-year-old daughter were caught in a gang shoot-out while crossing the playground. At the time of the interview, in December 1989, she reported, "The child still shakes when she hears a balloon break or some other loud noise."

Living in an environment of chronic violence may produce a range of responses, by one individual to a particular event, that change over time. For example, one mother has observed the reactions of her youngest daughter to shooting incidents. When she was two years old the girl was very frightened when she heard gunfire outside. She would literally hit the floor of the apartment, saying, "Mama, I'm scared," and she developed bad headaches and stomachaches following the incidents. Her mother took her to the doctor, and he confirmed that the physical symptoms were related to psychological stress felt by this child. He prescribed Tylenol. After a year, the mother noted that her daughter became "immune" to the shooting. The child's headaches and stomachaches ended, and when shooting started she told her mother, "Well, Mama, we have to get down on the floor."

Children as Perpetrators,
Perpetrators as Victims

The attack on a woman jogger in New York's Central Park by a gang of youth was an incident of "wilding," or violence as a planned activity. Following the incident, the media raised questions about whether this behavior was the result of youth being overexposed to violence in their lives. According to researchers, gangs influence the behavior of their members. "The rites of passage [for gang membership] include the commission of violent acts, including intimidation, assault, robbery, and murder" (Seever 1990). In interviews with mothers, we learned that children as young as nine are involved in illegal activity in their neighborhoods. They have observed older gang members organizing children to deliver drugs. When law officials are spotted in the neighborhood, gang members have been seen passing weapons, including automatic guns, to children, who place them in hiding. (Although minors can be prosecuted, they are less likely to receive time and are usually released to their parents' custody.) Children are victims of the adult organization associated with criminal activity.

During one four-month period in 1987 in Detroit, 102 children aged sixteen and younger were shot by other children (Zinsmeister 1990). Some young children demonstrate how violence influences decisions about allegiance and methods of defense against the violence. A Chicago policeman reported that he encountered a thirteen-year-old boy walking down the street with a .357 Magnum. The child was arrested. When asked why he had the gun, he replied that "he was afraid" (Blau 10 June 1990).

A mother who lives in public housing in Chicago described how she found a homemade gun in her five-year-old son's pocket. He had attempted to construct an Uzi with plastic and glue. When she asked him about the gun, he said that he needed it to protect himself from the gangs. Another mother said of her son, "He says his daddy will show him how to use a gun so he can shoot back."

In Detroit, a bullet killed six-year-old Christopher's best friend, his fifteen-year-old brother. Two years after his brother's murder, Christopher was asked by a reporter, "If you could have anything in the whole world, what would you want?" He responded, "A gun." She probed further, "What would you do with the gun?" Christopher said, "Blow the person's head off, who killed my brother" (Marin 1989).

Parenting

We interviewed parents in Chicago to increase our understanding of the problems they face, how they respond, and the resources they use to survive. Current public housing residents report that gang violence, especially in the context of drug sales and use, is their greatest concern, something they think about constantly. Parents who have moved out of public housing, without exception, told us that violence was the reason they left. Danger in the environment undermines their psychological well-being and affects every aspect of their lives.

The rules that parents give children reflect a preoccupation with safety. Children are instructed: "Don't go out in the hallway. Don't go around the corners. Stay away from windows. Don't watch the news [too violent]. Don't sit by the windows. Turn out the lights before you look out the window. If you hear shots, hit the floor. Don't walk by yourself. Go in and out quickly and don't bother anyone. Run and get out of the way [if shooting starts]. Stay together, all the time" (Dubrow and Garbarino 1989).

A school social worker told us that children are taught to observe gang members and identify whether they are carrying guns. If the children see guns, they are instructed to lie down, get under a slide on the playground, go to their own house or to a house of a familiar neighbor, and wait until it is safe to continue. One twelve-year-old girl echoed these rules, explaining to us, "When the shooting starts, and we're on the playground, we run inside." She added, "What am I supposed to do? Stand there and get shot?" (Ogintz 1989).

There are also safety rules inside the house. Children are taught to hide in designated safe places if they hear gunfire outside. One mother told us, "I always make them lay down on the floor, because a bullet could come in through the kitchen or living room windows, and ricochet, and hit one of us." Another mother confirmed this possibility. She said, "One day I was in the kitchen and I went to the refrigerator and a bullet came through my window and it hit here" (she pointed to a place in the middle of the wall between the floor and the ceiling). Still another parent told us that she and the children retreat to the hall closet until the shooting stops. These protective strategies are not exclusive to Chicago. They exist in high-crime inner-city areas across the country. For example, in Oakland, California, a grandmother taught her six-year-old granddaughter to get into the bathtub when shooting starts. Her rationale: "That's the safest place" (Gross 1990).

According to all the mothers we interviewed, living in public housing is like living in a prison. They told us that violence dictated their family schedules, activities, and diets. Decisions about buying groceries, doing laundry, or going to the park had to be weighed against the possible exposure to violence. Mothers reported that the threat of violence kept them from going out after dark.

As a protective strategy, mothers carried a week's purchase of groceries up seven flights of stairs to avoid a potentially dangerous elevator ride. According to one mother who lives in Cabrini Green, keeping yourself and your child in the house *all* the time is the only way to stay safe. Her two-year-old daughter cries to go outside, and she must say no. She said, "How can you explain to her? That you can't go outside to play because they're shooting?" One mother described how the simple chore of emptying the garbage can be dangerous: "I had just thrown out the garbage and came in. I heard this click, click, click. I go back to the door to see what it was. My brother said, 'Don't open that door, they just got through shooting.' I waited for a while and I'm sitting there trembling, thinking I just came into this door, it could have been me or you know it could have been my daughter." Another mother said that she was shot at while on her way to register her children at school. She estimated that the bullet missed her by a half inch. She said, "I was so scared, I wet on myself. It was embarrassing and frightening."

According to parents, coping with danger and observing its effects on children's behavior is extremely stressful. One mother said, "I try to stay strong in front of her, but I break down." Another said, "It would bring tears to my eyes, because I couldn't do any better." One mother challenged us: "Just think about the kids, what it does to them, living in fear of wondering if you're going to be shot or not."

Professionals

People who provide services to families in these communities are also at risk for crime victimization in the course of their day-to-day work. For example, one of the regional directors of the Illinois

Department of Children and Family Services reported that at any given time at least two of his one hundred caseworkers are unable to work because of injuries sustained while going to and coming from the homes of the families they serve. In a survey conducted by Erikson Institute, forty Head Start staff who worked in high-crime areas were asked to describe the things that happened around the children's center that made them fearful or upset. Over 60 percent of the staff had experienced shootings and gang-related activities and listed them as the things that caused them the most fear.

A Head Start social worker told us that on her way to conduct a home visit, she had to take cover to avoid being hit by random bullets fired by warring gang factions. She witnessed the shooting of one young man before the gunfire stopped. She waited until there were no more shots and ran back to the children's center. She reported the incident to a coworker, who listened sympathetically. The social worker said, "Then it was over." The next day she resumed her home visiting activities, constantly anticipating danger in the environment.

A group worker walked to the local elementary school to pick up children and escort them to the neighborhood afterschool program. On the way back to the center several youth chased them, wielding bats over their heads and threatening them with assault. The group worker and children ran as fast as they could to the center. Although they were not injured, the worker reported that the event was both frightening and stressful. These were also the reactions of another group worker who had to take cover in mid-afternoon when shooting started. She told us that she and the fifteen school-age children waited silently in a hallway until the shooting stopped and it was safe to return to the center. Still another Head Start worker was warned by community residents that two rival gangs were preparing to have a "shoot-out" in retaliation for a recent killing of one of their members. Staff contacted the children's parents, requesting that they come to the center and take the children home before the anticipated trouble began. All the children were picked up, except one. When the shooting started, all of the teachers and the one child huddled in an inner stairway of the school until the gunfire stopped. The director of the program requested special mental health services for the staff and the child, because the event was so distressing to everyone involved.

The shooting death of a four-year-old Head Start child prompted the staff to ask for special help to deal with difficult emotions aroused by the event. Unfortunately, it was not the first time they had confronted loss and separation between themselves and young students as the result of community violence. However, as the director explained, "This was the straw that broke the camel's back."

Local public school staff who work in high-crime communities are also exposed to the violent deaths and injuries of their students. For one elementary school teacher, whose school served a local public housing development, the task of cleaning out her students' desks after they had died violently occurred three times in one school year.

Is There Any End to the War at Home?

"Violence is not something you get used to. Just because you're in an environment laced with violence doesn't mean it's an okay way of life" (quoted in Ogintz 1989).

Is there societal concern for these children of war? A recent media report equates the chronic violence of one of the nation's high-crime urban ghettos to three war zones of the world: "Child Warriors: Afghanistan, Northern Ireland, Burma, and Los Angeles" (Stanley 1990). We have found that the comparison of gang-controlled communities to war zones serves to emphasize the traumatic nature of experiences with life-threatening events, which are unpredictable, uncontrollable, and overwhelming. It is here, however, where the comparison begins to fall apart.

Individuals who live in a war zone have an identifiable enemy and a sense that the conflict, no matter how long it has been going on, is essentially a temporary state of affairs that will end once the conflict is resolved. They also receive societal support for their suffering, and they generally live within a community united by its aims and strong cultural traditions. It is this support and validation that enables individuals to cope with the impact of war and to maintain family and cultural ties despite intense stress and suffering. They can develop a personal and collective narrative that makes sense out of the horror they confront. They can find a political meaning in struggle. They can take solace in ideology.

In gang-controlled communities the enemy is not so easily identified. Is it the young mother on drugs, the older brother who is a gang member, or the police who fail to respond to calls for help? Parents admit their confusion over whom to trust, and recognize that they cannot consistently identify the enemy in public housing environments. In interviews with mothers who left Chicago Housing Authority (CHA) apartments, we learned that one mother called the person who murdered her cousin a friend. The man was a neighbor, someone she knew in her youth. She described him as a good person. However, as he got older, he became involved in local gang activity, and he killed her cousin. She said, "Do you know how hard it is to think about a murderer who is a good person?"

Mothers live in communities where gang members act without concern for children. One mother, who still lives in a CHA building, described a shooting incident in which rival gang members volleyed gunfire at each other near a school bus that was picking up a group of second-grade children. When we asked whether she thought the gangs saw the children in their line of fire, she said, "They see them; they don't care. All they care about is themselves. Their own kids could be out there, and they'll start shooting; their own mama could be out there."

One mother, who had left public housing, described how difficult it is for the police and CHA security to maintain law and order in the projects. She observed, "When something happens, everyone claims to see nothing; to give information to the police might mean informing on a neighbor or a relative." For a mother who lives in Cabrini Green, reporting crime translates into trouble for the entire family. She said, "If you testify against a gang-banger, that gives him a chance to come and kill you before the court day or harass someone in your family. You're going to have to move, and you don't have nowhere to go. So, what you do, you just shut up."

Since there is little perceived societal support for the people trapped in these communities, the ability to unite around common goals and maintain families and cultural ties is weak. Instead, residents experience a unique form of physical and psychological stress that becomes an assault on one's self-esteem that is not recognized by society and is only vaguely comprehended by the residents themselves. As a result, residents receive little external validation for their experience or recognition of their efforts to cope with the situation.

Because the enemy remains faceless, active coping mechanisms and communitywide response are undermined. To survive, every person must exert considerable energy to deal with this assault.

One mother gave an account of drug sales in Cabrini Green: "It's so open. If I see it, and my kids see it, the police see it. It seems to me as though the policemen want this to happen." She perceives the lack of support as intentional in a plan to reclaim valuable land on which public housing has been built. She continued, "If the poor keep on killing each other [over drugs], then they'll [the rich] have less to move out."

Some people break out of the prison, but it is an arduous process, as we learned in the interviews with mothers who left their public housing environments. People leave because of violence, gangs, and drugs. They also described major breakdowns in the management of CHA buildings: poor maintenance, lack of security, illegal persons present on the property (specifically related to gang activity), and breakdown of internal monitoring systems developed by the residents themselves. Many of the women had lived in public housing for ten years and lamented the fact that the community was once a safer and more positive place to live. They resent having to become refugees from their homes just as much as the refugees we met in Nicaragua, and Cambodia, and Mozambique, and Palestine.

We asked, "How did you select where to move?" Fifty percent of the mothers told us they had moved in with other family members. Staying close to family was a major factor in the selection of a new residence. Seventy percent of the mothers thought that the new home was better than their public housing apartment. When we asked mothers what made it difficult to leave housing, the overwhelming response was money. With extremely limited incomes, getting money for rent deposit, utility services charges, and moving vans was very difficult. What has a safer environment cost these women? One mother reported that at the time of the move her wardrobe consisted of two blouses, one pair of jeans, one pair of canvas gym shoes, and one sweatshirt. We thought of a mother in Cambodia who told the same story about her efforts to flee the Khmer Rouge and of the grandmother in Nicaragua whose story of fleeing the Contras echoed this account.

Another mother explained, "Saving money out of a public aid check only takes one thing: sacrifice, sacrifice, sacrifice." For example, from a monthly public aid check of $385, one of the women reported paying $250 per month on rent plus utilities. The apartment she rented for herself and her two children has no locks on the door and is rat-infested. Transportation, clothing, and other expenses come from the balance of $135.00 per month. She feels she is teetering on the edge of homelessness. She may be forced to return to the dangerous environment of public housing.

In any American community, there are friends, family, and elements of self-determination that bolster efforts to make life better. The adults and children we met constantly juggle the question: should we stay in the situation, or should we leave it and begin again? It is a difficult dilemma, one that those who live in a war zone always face, knowing that a mistake can be fatal.

To Feel Safe, to Be Safe

What is truly needed in America's urban war zones is restoration of a safe environment where children can have a childhood, and where parents can exert less energy on protecting children from random gunfire and more on helping children to grow. No one can eliminate all risk from the lives of families. But America does have the resources to make a real childhood a real possibility even for the children of the urban poor. But sometimes the war close to home is the most difficult to see.

Young children are being exposed to chronic violence at an alarming rate in the United States. There is growing concern among professionals that the war zones of the world are not limited to places characterized by armed conflict in the traditional sense. For example, in isolated inner-city communities of the United States, violent crimes committed by rival gang members are a primary source of danger to children. Public housing developments in large cities such as Chicago, New York, and Detroit house thousands of children. These environments are considered to be some of the highest-crime communities in the world. Environmental danger of this magnitude is equaled only in the lives of children who live in situations of armed conflict. Time and further study will tell this story more completely than we can at present, but we fear that the war at home may turn out to be as costly as any we have ever fought abroad—win or lose.

In one afterschool program in a Chicago public housing development that we visited, the children played funeral every day for weeks. They would build a casket with blocks and take turns lying in the casket. The children took on roles of preacher, family members, and mourners. They would weep and cry out for the person who died, saying, "Don't take him!" Who will bring peace to these children?

8

Making a Place for Children Who Have No Place to Be a Child

Looking at the children of war zones reminded us that some of the worst consequences of today's wars are not physical and psychological, but social. Wars produce social dislocation, of which one consequence is a breakdown in the basic "infrastructure of life." All too often this includes food, health care, and education.

In Nicaragua and in Mozambique, for example, we found thousands of children who had fled with their families to the major cities to escape day-to-day danger in their home regions. The result in both cases was shantytown living. In Cambodia and in the Middle East war has meant *generations* of children growing up in refugee camps. In Chicago, the "war" drives out those who can afford to leave, just the kind of people who are needed to improve the social climate. Thus, it produces ever greater concentrations of poor, psychologically needy people who are angry, depressed, or angry and depressed, people who are stuck in place.

The economic crises that accompany and flow from war often mean severe food shortages—and shortages of cash to buy food. Inadequate nutrition at best, and malnutrition at worst, are usually associated with war. In Mozambique, doctors report a massive increase in malnutrition. We visited a ward in Maputo Hospital where they cared for the most serious cases of malnutrition. Whereas other children in the hospital had been lively and responsive to the hand puppets we brought to entertain them, here we found apathy. One child in particular caught our attention. She was tiny for her age, and her chart revealed that she was being treated for five separate deficiency diseases. Her mother had been widowed in a Renamo attack, and the surviving family had fled to the city in search of a more secure place to live. They found military security but no protection from a new poverty more pernicious than what they had known in the countryside. The little girl's grim expression and guarded watchfulness were impervious to us and our puppets. No bullet or bomb had wounded her, but she was a victim of war as much as any of the others we saw.

In most third world countries war means malnutrition and famine. And it means mass migration to cities whose economic resources and ability to supply services are already overtaxed. The children of war become the desperately poor children living in shantytowns, the desperately weak and sick children in the hospital wards, and the traumatized children in homes, clinics, and residential institutions. Even in the urban war zones of America, despite our affluent society, infant mortality and morbidity are much higher than in safer neighborhoods, and poor health and malnutrition are disproportionately common.

The children of war are disproportionately poor to start with. Social class does not take a vacation in a war zone. War always hits the poor hardest. The rich have the resources to protect themselves and their children, and to flee to safety if the war comes too close. And who can blame them for that? No parent certainly.

Look Straight On, Don't Turn Away

It is hard to look at the children of war. Even the success stories tend to remind you of the wastage, to highlight what is lost to so many. Being willing to see clearly the costs of war to children is the first step. Doing something about it is the next step.

On 3 April 1990, the U.S. Senate Subcommittee on Children held a hearing on "Children in War" under the chairmanship of Senator Christopher Dodd. UNICEF's goodwill ambassador, actress Liv Ullmann, testified as an expert witness based upon her experiences visiting with child victims of war around the world. After she had finished, and while other witnesses were offering their observations, analysis, and recommendations, she turned to Jim (who was sitting next to her awaiting his turn to testify) and said, "Does anyone listen to all these words? Does anyone do anything as a result of all this?"

Is anyone listening? *Does* anyone do anything? Knowledge and analysis are crucial, of course. As we noted earlier, a wise person once said, "You can change the world. But unless you know what you are doing . . . please don't!" Doing without understanding can lead to disaster. Seeking knowledge for its own sake can be beautiful—in aesthetics, pure science, and philosophy, for example. But with the children of war, knowing can only be redeemed by doing. Knowing without doing is obscene.

So what are we to do?

First, we must take care of the children of war. To care for them, we must put aside political labels and get on with the business of helping. We must address the needs of children of war without regard for their political ideology or the ideology of their parents. Children who are victims of war are a "side" that we must always support. Even in Chicago.

The war in Chicago casts many children as actors in the conflict. Most are witnesses. Many are victims. Some become perpetrators. What do we do for these children? Mostly nothing. When a crazed woman entered an affluent suburban school and shot several children (one fatally), the story was front-page news for a long time. Two days later, a little boy was shot in the head and arm in the Chicago war zone. The story appeared as one paragraph on page 22. Teams of psychologists, psychiatrists, and social workers were mobilized in the affluent suburb, and a year later they were still providing therapy to some of the children and their families. In the urban war zone, where more than one in four children witnesses a homicide, children and parents are on their own. Their situation is more like Cambodia than it is like the suburbs.

During the hearing at which Liv Ullmann asked her pointed question, testimony was presented about the insufficiency of resources to deal with the problems of refugee children. Afghans flee to Pakistan and Iran. Somalis and Sudanese flee to Ethiopia. Salvadorans flee to Nicaragua. Mozambicans flee to Zambia. Cambodians flee to Thailand. The numbers are large and growing.

According to United Nations estimates, more than 15 million people have been forced to flee across national frontiers to other countries in search of safety and a chance to live in peace (Berry-Koch 1990). In addition, millions more are internal refugees. The problems of refugees are intrinsically political. As we have seen, governments and other political actors use refugees as pawns in their power struggles (Mullen 1988).

Refugees include fathers, mothers, and millions of children. According to the UN high commissioner for refugees, the swelling numbers of refugees have not been accompanied by a proportionate increase in UN resources (Berry-Koch 1990). Today the UN's refugee effort must operate with only 25 percent of the per person resources it had in 1980. As a result, many young refugee children are suffering from malnutrition even though they are officially in the "care" of the international community. The international refugee problem parallels the situation of the homeless in America, who often find the public resources available to them meager at best. Those who find themselves homeless must often resort to illegal means to find the money to survive. In many American communities the amount of money made available as "welfare" for the poor is insufficient for them to make ends meet without cheating.

Psychological First Aid for Children

Individually and through our collective political and philanthropic voices we must do something to increase the resources available for aiding refugee children, whatever their politics. For children who still have their parents, supporting families and seeking to relocate or repatriate them in safety should be the strategy of choice. For children who have lost their parents, we must find ways to create new homes and families for them as soon as possible. These efforts might be categorized as psychological first aid programs. By supporting children who have their parents we will enable most of them to hold on to a positive reality. First aid is about safety, and the most important elements of safety to children of war are—in order of importance—parents, kin, home, and prospects for the future.

Consider the case of Eritrea, whose people have been fighting a war to secede from Ethiopia for years. One recent study has begun to look at the development of two groups of children who live within a few miles of each other (Wolff 1990). The first group consists of orphans who live together in an orphanage–refugee camp under appalling conditions. The second group consists of children who live with their parents in a refugee camp under equally appalling conditions. The first group of children exhibits high levels of disabilities and psychopathology. The second group is managing to cope and stay on track developmentally—at least in contrast to the orphaned group. How often must we be taught this lesson before we change the way we treat orphaned children?

We must work to knit together the world that has been torn apart by war. If children are separated from parents, our first goal should be to reunite them. If children have been orphaned, our first goal should be to reunite them with kin. If loving kin are unavailable, then our goal should be the creation of a new family for the child through foster parents, adoption, or even long-term group living.

Beyond First Aid

Some children will need more than psychological first aid. What can we do beyond first aid? We can support programs designed to offer long-term therapy and rehabilitation for the children of war. If their experiences have been deeply traumatic, they will need emotional and behavioral rehabilitation. If they suffer from clinically diagnosed post traumatic stress disorder, they will need psychiatric intervention.

This need is most evident in war zones such as Mozambique and Cambodia (and perhaps Chicago), where children have been drawn into horrible experiences as combatants. But the need is also evident elsewhere, where children have constructed life-styles that are an attempt to make sense of the distorted world of a war zone, and as a result need help having a second crack at childhood. In Nicaragua, efforts have been made to help smooth the psychic rehabilitation of traumatized children. In Chicago, some few brave therapists like psychiatrist Carl Bell have sought ways to help children cope with community violence. The lack of resources commensurate with the task is appalling, particularly because nations that could help always manage to find enough money to pay for more armaments.

An International Commitment
to the Human Rights of Children

We as Americans must embrace the letter and spirit of the United Nations Convention on the Rights of the Child (Cohen and Davidson 1990). Article 38 states in part:

1. Parties should undertake to respect and ensure respect for rules of international humanitarian law applicable to them in armed conflicts which are relevant to the child.
2. Parties shall take all feasible measures to ensure that persons who have not attained the age of fifteen years do not take a direct part in hostilities.
3. Parties shall refrain from recruiting any person who has not attained the age of fifteen years into their armed forces. In recruiting among those persons who have attained the age of fifteen years but who have not attained the age of eighteen years, Parties shall endeavor to give priority to those who are oldest.
4. In accordance with their obligations under international humanitarian law to protect the civilian population in armed conflicts, Parties shall take all feasible measures to ensure protection and care of children who are affected by an armed conflict.

Article 39 states that parties shall take all appropriate measures to promote physical and psychological recovery and social reintegration of a child victim of any form of neglect, exploitation, or abuse; torture or any other form of cruel, inhuman, or degrading treatment or punishment; or armed conflict. Such recovery and reintegration shall take place in an environment that fosters the health, self-respect, and dignity of the child.

What does all this mean? It means that the international community is seeking a way to create a protected space for children, for childhood, even in the midst of war. It means that every nation should accept and live by the concept of "limited war." And it means that when children and childhood are violated by armed conflict, the countries involved should make whatever amends are possible.

Less clear is what the UN convention means for nationalist uprisings, situations in which the entire population rises up against an unrepresentative government or an occupying foreign power. How does the convention apply to what happened in Eastern Europe as the 1980s closed, as millions of citizens of all ages refused to be governed by Communist parties that did not represent them? What does it mean for the Palestinian *Intifada,* where children and youth have been the vanguard in resisting Israeli occupation? Some people think there are easy and clear answers, and that they themselves have those answers. We are not so sure.

The UN convention contains provisions that seek to guarantee a wide range of rights to children, including rights to free expression and association, the right to a nationality, and the right to be free from attacks on the individual child's "honor and reputation." How does one square these rights with living under foreign occupation? How does one reconcile these rights with living in a totalitarian state? How consonant are these rights with being a member of a subjugated ethnic minority? How can these rights coexist with life in the inner city wracked by festering issues of race and social class?

The generally recognized universal right to self-determination runs through and underlies much of the thinking that went into the UN Convention on the Rights of the Child. A careful and sympathetic analysis must be made of each situation of nationalist uprising in which children and youth are participants to come to a judgment that respects *all* the rights of the child. It is our challenge to balance a child's right to safety with a democratic society's commitment to civil rights.

It is clear to us that adults on both sides of a nationalist uprising have a responsibility to go the extra mile in establishing special standards for the conduct of armed conflicts in which children are involved and in doing all they can after the conflict is resolved to restore to those children whatever they have sacrificed in the name of the nation for which they have struggled. Even in the urban war zone; even in the drug war.

No UN convention automatically makes a significant contribution to improving the world unless it becomes a document that lives in the minds and hearts of governments and citizens. The UN Convention on the Rights of the Child is no exception. It does contain a mechanism for monitoring implementation, but that mechanism could become a hollow shell, a formalistic sham, unless the world's leaders take it seriously.

In September and October 1990 more world leaders than had ever before attended a summit meeting traveled to New York for the United Nations Summit on Children. They pledged to meet the commitments laid out in the Convention on the Rights of the Child. Will they "do the right thing"?

Many observers recognized the irony of holding such a meeting in an American city in which infant mortality in poor neighborhoods exceeds that found in some third world countries. Will the United States apply the convention to the war zone at home? Will we do the right thing?

What will it take to ensure that this happens, that public officials do take the convention seriously? They must believe that their citizens take it seriously and will hold them accountable. It's a matter of information and belief: information about what is really happening and belief that what does happen should meet moral standards. Americans have a special responsibility, particularly since as the World Summit on Children met and as we wrote these words the United States was one of the few countries in the world lagging behind in ratifying it.

Is There a Place for War in the Moral World of Children?

Christian theologians developed the concept of the "just war." They did so in an effort to distinguish between "good wars" and "bad wars." Why was this necessary? It served to provide combatants with a justification for suspending the commandment not to kill (which was never intended to prohibit war at all, but simply to limit killing within the group).

Christians usually have the blessing of their faith when they march off to war. Moslems have their "holy wars," which offer special benefits to the fighters and the victims of wars fought on behalf of Allah. How convenient it all is that some clergyman is always available to provide a blessing for slaughter. How sad it is that so few bear witness for peace.

We met a five-year-old Palestinian child in a refugee camp near Nablus. He had been hit in the head with a rubber bullet the day before. Although he had been taken to the hospital, there was nothing health professionals could do for him. He lay in his mother's arms, groggy, eyes glazed, surrounded by family and neighbors. We tried later to find out what had happened to him. We were told he had died—he was a martyr they said. Someone who ought to know better is always around to justify the death of a child for some higher purpose. Have we no shame?

A Continuum of Bestiality

As much as we hate to accept gradations of evil, we must acknowledge that in looking at the wars of this world, it *does* seem that there is a continuum of bestiality. There are gradations of the horrible. Indeed, one criterion for assessing the barbarism with which a war is being fought is by determining the condition of the children touched by the war. Another is determining the degree to which the killing and maiming is done "humanely," bizarre as that seems.

Cambodia and Mozambique are at the extreme end of whatever scale it is we are describing. In Cambodia it is recognized that the Khmer Rouge exceeded any and all limitations. The depravity of the slaughter was reminiscent of Christian Europe's worst acts of barbarism: the Crusades, medieval religious wars, and the Holocaust of World War II.

In Mozambique, Renamo's tactics likewise have been barbaric in the extreme. Were they in power one wonders what inventive use they might make of wanton slaughter. Perhaps they would follow the example set by the Khmer Rouge. Perhaps not. But the wantonness and inventiveness of their cruelty provides a firm foundation for dreading the worst.

Nicaragua has had its share of baseness. Contras locking four young sisters into the house in which they had just slaughtered their father and mother is barbaric according to any moral system. But the Contras are not in the same league as Cambodia's Khmer Rouge and Mozambique's Renamo.

Closer to the human end of the continuum is the Palestinian *Intifada*. It is truly a "limited war" in many respects, on both sides. This matters. It matters in moral accounting. And it matters in its effects on the participants. The conflict is often terrible, often characterized by wanton and gratuitous brutality. But it has a political structure that leaves room for moral discourse between the combatants. It leaves room for children. Even though it violates standards of good conduct repeatedly, as conflicts go it is quite restrained—on both sides. We say this even as things deteriorated in the wake of the Temple Mount/Haram al-Sharif killings in October 1990.

Indeed, what horrifies us most about the war in Chicago is the suspicion that rules for the combatants are deteriorating. The killing becomes steadily more casual, and more bestial. Drugs drive and accelerate this process. A mother who was nearly shot cries out, "They don't care about nothin' anymore. They'd shoot their own mother if she got in their way." When the war is beyond caring, the slide to barbarism is often precipitous.

Limited War

Perhaps it is this matter of limiting the war that defines the essence of the moral continuum we seek. When there are no standards beyond what is technically feasible and what is presumed to have the desired effects, then the door is opened to the limitless barbarism of the Khmer Rouge and Renamo.

Others may find our conclusion repugnant, but we must acknowledge that there is a detectable moral distinction between a father or brother being shot in the course of an active confrontation, and a father or a brother being beheaded "in cold blood."

And there is also, we presume, a psychological distinction to be drawn for a child who witnesses the first act versus a child who witnesses the second. The minimal hope of international child advocates is that the world's combatants will start with these distinctions and build upon them until no child is a victim of war.

A good place to start would be to insist that civilians are "off limits" to warring parties. We as Americans should learn this simple and effective moral lesson. During late 1990 and early 1991 the United States moved toward its war against Iraq, war in the form of massive bombing of Bagdhad and other population centers. When Fascist armies bombed civilians during the Spanish Civil War in the 1930s, the world was outraged. The fact that bombing civilians seems to be accepted today as an obvious strategy should fill us with horror and make us recoil to recognize how far we have regressed in this century to the barbarous past when sacking the enemy's cities was a matter of course. The degeneration of gang warfare in the cities seems to parallel the degeneration of our warring beyond our national borders.

Bringing Home the Rights of the Child in War

Implicitly and explicitly, the UN Convention on the Rights of the Child calls upon us to take a good hard look at how our government's policies and practices affect children, particularly children in the context of war situations. We also have a moral responsibility to examine the efforts of private citizens and public figures who support governments and organizations that make war on children.

For example, the Mozambique Support Network has compiled a list of individuals and groups in the United States who support Renamo, and thus its campaign of unmitigated and bestial attacks on civilians in Mozambique. The 1990 list included members of the House of Representatives, senators, and religious leaders. All seemed to think that Renamo deserved their support because it proclaimed itself antiCommunist and pro-Christian. But could these ends, even if true, justify Renamo's means?

What can we do? For a start, we can take responsibility for our own government's military actions and policies that affect children. Every military action has direct and indirect implications for the lives and well-being of children. This truth should be clear to anyone. When our soldiers kill other people's soldiers, they kill fathers and brothers. When civilians are killed "accidentally" in the cross fire or intentionally as part of attacks on "infrastructure," children and their mothers are victims.

We know that "projecting military force" leads to child casualties—whether they be the passengers on an Iranian airliner "accidentally" shot down over the Persian Gulf or "innocent bystanders" killed in Panama. Oh yes, we know that "their side" is worse. But whose side are we on? And for whom are we responsible? Whose side were we on in Cambodia when the Khmer Rouge massacred so many fellow Cambodians? Whose side were we on in Vietnam when our allies routinely tortured and summarily executed prisoners, and we supported indiscriminate bombing in the countryside?

But the casualties for which we are directly responsible because of our military actions are not our only responsibility. Every day around the world children are hurt by weapons manufactured in the United States. Some of these weapons are sold by private American businesses. Others are paid for by taxpayers and given away by our government as part of our geopolitical policy.

We cannot hide behind disclaimers of free enterprise, the right to bear arms, or "strategic considerations." If you want peace, you must work for justice.

We are responsible. What do you say when fourteen-year-olds can go out on the town armed with a revolver? What do you say when a mother brings her dead child to you and asks why a fourteen-year-old can buy a gun on the street with his allowance? What do you say when you travel to a village and a parent brings forth the weapon that killed her child and clearly marked on it are the words "Made in the U.S.A.?" How do you answer the question of the grieving mother who asks, "Why do you do this? Why?"

Oh yes, we know that other countries are worse than we are. But pointing to worse offenders does not relieve us of our responsibilities. In every war zone we visited—including the inner city of Chicago—there is an American interest and presence. We are responsible. We virtually created the Contras in Nicaragua. We ostracized the "Marxist" government of Mozambique and tolerated the efforts of white Rhodesia and South Africa to create and supply Renamo. We fought a secret war in Cambodia that ironically permitted the Khmer Rouge to take over, and then did nothing to stop them when they began their program. When the Vietnamese invaded and overthrew them, we continued to turn our backs as a way of taking revenge for our "defeat" in the Vietnam War and to placate our Chinese friends who favored the Khmer Rouge. In Chicago, generations of policies designed to perpetuate racial and class disparities have combined with a cowboy ethic of gun-toting violence to produce the horrors we encounter today. In the Middle East we are right in the thick of the Israeli-Palestinian conflict.

We are responsible.

Casualties Beyond the Casualties

And even these casualties are not the whole story. Deployment of military force ripples through the lives of children in many other ways besides physical injury. Every military deployment means children become parentless. In the first few months of the American deployment in Saudi Arabia in response to the "Gulf Crisis," some members of our armed forces died before even a shot was fired by them or their comrades in arms. Flying planes and driving tanks and carrying weapons and handling military cargo is a dangerous business even without fighting.

But even this is not all. Thousands of American children experience the wrench of attachments frequently and repeatedly disrupted because their fathers (or increasingly their mothers) are military personnel. As military personnel they get assigned to duty that involves long periods of separation from family members. And in today's armed forces, one out of ten soldiers is a woman, some of them mothers.

The U.S. military now recognizes—at least in principle—that "you recruit individuals but you retain families," and is developing a wide variety of family support programs in an attempt to minimize the threat to emotional well-being posed by military service. As massive deployment of American soldiers to the Gulf in 1990 brought about massive family disruption, the Pentagon scrambled to find counselors who could step in to help pick up the pieces with thousands of "abandoned" children.

But the fact remains that one consequence of maintaining military forces is that children lose their parents for extended periods even if there is never a shot fired in earnest. It may seem an indulgence, a luxury of sorts, to worry about these "children of war" when there are children bleeding and mourning because of what soldiers do. But it is part of the story, if only a minor chapter in the grand scheme of things.

Now That We Know, What Will We Do?

Once we know what is happening, what are we to do about it? One concrete step would be to pass legislation requiring a "child impact analysis" for all military spending and policy: the sale of arms, the giving of military aid, direct military action undertaken by our armed forces, and even the deployment of our armed forces within and outside our national borders. And we could extend this model to include urban policy that affects the problem of community violence at home.

What happens to children because we sell antipersonnel weapons to governments who then use them to suppress rural insurgencies? What happens when we arm or politically endorse a resistance movement that attacks civilian populations in an effort to weaken the national government? What happens when we allow guns to flood poor inner-city neighborhoods as if selling and buying them were morally equivalent to buying and selling kitchen appliances? What happens when we base soldiers in a poor country, spreading venereal disease and providing a market for prostitution that includes not just mothers but children as well? We have an obligation to know that we have done all these things, that we continue to do all these things, that we will continue to do all these things unless we stop.

And what if we did know?

The war in American cities goes on and on, with new records being set for homicide and assault. Forty countries are at war in the world today (UNICEF 1990). The Iraqi invasion of Kuwait raised the prospect and then brought to fruition a new and very big war.

Some would argue that requiring a "child impact analysis" for all military and urban action and policy would be "counterproductive" because it would force an end to war. "If people had to confront the reality of what war at home and abroad really means for children, they couldn't stomach it. It's only the protective fiction of 'not knowing' that permits it all to continue." Perhaps. But isn't that precisely why we ought to start now? If not now, when? If not us, who?

Postscript

"**N**ow that I know, what can I do?"

People often say this to us after they have heard our story of children growing up in war zones. What can one person do? We think everyone can do something. Becoming better informed about the issues, and about American policy in each war zone, is one thing to do. Contributing to the organizations that employ and support the healers and the peacemakers is another.

We have some suggestions for each of the war zones about which we have written, suggestions that we are committed to updating as conditions change. For a list of these suggestions, please write us at Erikson Institute, 25 West Chicago Avenue, Chicago, Illinois 60610.

References

Abu-Lughod, J. (1971). Demographic transformation of Palestine. In Ibrahim Abu-Lughod, *Transformation of Palestine*, 139–163. Evanston, IL: Northwestern University Press.

Acker, A. (1986). *Children of the volcano*. Westport, CT: Lawrence Hill & Co.

African Kora. Journal of Artists and Intellectuals for Children. (1990, March–April). 2(2).

Amnesty International. (1989). *Nicaragua: The human rights record, 1986–1989*. New York: Amnesty International Publications.

Association of Israeli and Palestinian Physicians. Medical care impeded by the Israeli authorities as a tool of political pressure. *DataBase Project on Palestinian Human Rights*, 1 January 1989, 20.

Bangkok Post. (1990, July 21). Khmer Rouge ready and willing to fight long war.

Bell, C., & Jenkins, J. (Forthcoming). Traumatic stress and children in danger. *Journal of Health Care for the Poor and Underserved*.

Berry-Koch, A. (1990, April 3). The consequences of displacement. Testimony presented to the U.S. Senate Committee on Labor and Human Resources.

Bettelheim, B. (1943). Individual and mass behavior in extreme situations. *Journal of Abnormal and Social Psychology, 38*, 417–452.

Bishop, P. (1989, January 23). Palestinian children are main victims of Israelis. *Daily Telegraph* (London), 1.

Blau, R. (1990, April 6). Child in wrong place at wrong time is blinded. *Chicago Tribune*, sec. 2, 1.

Blau, R. (1990, June 10). Gang violence defies any easy answers. *Chicago Tribune*, 1, 5.

Boothby, N. (1990, June). *Working in the war zone: A look at psychological theory and practice from the field*. Paper presented at the Children and War Conference, Hebrew University, Jerusalem.

Bronowski, J. (1973). *The ascent of man*. Boston: Little, Brown & Company.

Burns, J. (1990, February 4). Afgans: Now they blame America. *New York Times*, sec. 6.

Caseso, J., & Blau, R. (1989, June 18). Fear lives in CHA's Taylor Homes. *Chicago Tribune*, 1, 16.

Chicago Housing Authority, Department of Grants and Statistical Information. (1990). Staff interview.

Chicago Housing Authority, Office of Planning, Research, and Development. (1985). *1984/85 Statistical Report*. Chicago: Chicago Housing Authority.

Chicago Tribune. (1989, August 10). Guns, explosives seized in CHA high-rise sweeps, sec. 2, 2.

Chicago Tribune. (1990, November 19). Israel to curb buses, advertising, 8.

Chilton, R. (1987). Twenty years of homicide and robbery in Chicago: The impact of the city's changing racial and age composition. *Journal of Quantitative Criminology, 3*(3), 195–214.

Cockburn, A. (1990, November). Danny who? *Nation, 19*, 586–587.

Cohen, C. P., & Davidson, H. (Eds.). (1990). *Children's rights in America: U.N. Convention on the Rights of the Child compared with United States law*. Washington, DC: American Bar Association.

Coles, R. (1982). *The political life of children*. Boston: Houghton Mifflin.

Cravioto, J. (1966). *Pre-school child malnutrition*. Washington, DC: National Academy of Science and Natural Resources Council, chap. 7.

DataBase Project on Palestinian Human Rights. (1989a). *Children imprisoned*. Chicago: DataBase Project on Palestinian Human Rights.

DataBase Project on Palestinian Human Rights. (1989b). *Uprising in Palestine: The first year*. Chicago: DataBase Project on Palestinian Human Rights.

DeAngelis, T. (1990, July). Cambodians' sight loss tied to seeing atrocities. *APA Monitor, 36ff.*

Dubrow, N., & Garbarino, J. (1989, January–February). Living in the war zone: Mothers and young children in a public housing development. *Child Welfare* LXVIII (1).

Dyson, J. (1989). Family violence and its effect on children's academic under-achievement and behavior problems in school. *Journal of the National Medical Association* 82(1): 17–22.

Edelman, M. (1987). *Families in peril: An agenda for social change*. Cambridge: Harvard University Press.

Erikson, E. (1963). *Childhood and society*. New York: W. W. Norton & Company.

Finkelhor, D. (1984). *Child sexual abuse*. New York: Free Press.

Fish-Murray, C. (1990, October 10). Memories of trauma: Place and path. Keynote presentation, NAIM Foundation Conference on Children and Trauma, Washington, DC.

Freud, A., & Burlingham, D. (1943). *War and children*. New York: Ernest Willard.

Gannon, J. (1989, July 18). Two sides to a popular uprising. *Christian Science Monitor*, 1–2.

Garbarino, J., & Associates. (1982). *Children and families in the social environment*. New York: Aldine.

Garbarino, J., Stott, F., & Faculty of the Erikson Institute. (1989). *What children can tell us.* San Francisco: Jossey-Bass.

Gardner, G. (1971). Aggression and violence: The enemies of precision learning in children. *American Journal of Psychiatry 128*(4), 445–450.

Garmezy, N. (1990, June). War and children. An address presented at the Children and War Conference, Hebrew University, Jerusalem.

Greenberg, J., & J. Brilliant (1988, October 15). Riot death toll rises. *Jerusalem Post,* 1.

Gross, J. (1990, August 12). Bystander deaths reshape city lives. *New York Times,* 14.

Horton, M. (1990). *The long haul: An autobiography.* New York: Doubleday.

Illinois Criminal Justice Information Authority 1983 Report (1986). In Staff of the *Chicago Tribune* (Eds.), *The American millstone.* Chicago: Contemporary Books.

Jackson, R., & Kelly, H. (1945). Growth charts for use in pediatric practice. *Journal of Pediatrics, 27,* 215–229.

Janis, I. (1951). *Air war and emotional stress.* New York: McGraw Hill.

Jerusalem Post (1988, November 25).

Jerusalem Post (1989, February 8).

Karnow, S. (1983). Vietnam: A history. New York: Viking Press.

Kiernan, B. (1990). Roots of genocide: New evidence on the U. S. bombardment of Cambodia. *Cultural Survival Quarterly, 14*(3), 20–22.

Kifner, J. (1989, January 14). Israel uses new bullet against Arabs. *New York Times,* sec. A, 4.

Kinzer, S. (1988, January 28). Broken children, a truth of Nicaragua's war. *New York Times,* A1–A4.

Kinzie, J. D., Sack, W. H., Angell, R. H., Manson, S., & Rath, B. (1986). The psychiatric effects of massive trauma on Cambodian children. *Journal of the American Academy of Child Psychiatry, 25,* 370–376.

Kotulak, R. (1990, September 28). Study finds inner-city kids live with violence. *Chicago Tribune,* 1, 16.

Lane, C., & Padgett, T. (1990, November 26). The return of the Contras? *Newsweek,* 49.

Lösel, F., & Bliesener, T. (1990). Resilience in adolescence: A study on the generalizability of protective factors. In K. Hurrelmann & F. Losel (Eds.), *Health hazards in adolescence,* 299–320. New York: Walter de Gruter.

McCallin, M. (1989, August). *The impact of traumatic events on the psychological well-being of Mozambican reguee women and children.* Geneva, Switzerland: International Catholic Child Bureau.

McMullen, M. (1990, April–May). Activists observe elections, plan future action. *Peace and Justice Journal, 9.*

Marin, C. (1989, June 21). *Grief's children.* WMAQ (Chicago) TV documentary.

Mateus, M. (1990). Unpublished story. Province of Inhambane, Mozambique.

Metraux, J. (1988). *Guerra y desarrollo psicosocial de los ninos en los asentamientos de rio san juan.* Managua, Nicaragua: Editorial Vanguardia.

Metraux, J. (1990, June). Towards the definition of a model of preventive action directed to the children victims of war and their families. Paper presented at the Children and War Conference, Hebrew University, Jerusalem.

Morganthau, T. (1989, September 11). Children of the underclass. *Newsweek,* 16–32.

Mullen, W. (1988, October 9). No place called home. *Chicago Tribune Magazine,* sec. 10, 12ff.

National Association of Housing Redevelopment Officials. (1989). *The many faces of public housing.* Washington, DC: National Association of Housing.

Nelson, H. (1989, January 1). Nicaragua struggles to aid its children. *Los Angeles Times, 6.*

New York Times. (1989, January 18). 1:20

Nixon, A. (1990). *The status of Palestinian children during the uprising in the occupied territories.* Parts 1 and 2. East Jerusalem: Rädda Barnen.

Ogintz, E. (1989, May 24). Wounded childhood. *Chicago Tribune, Tempo,* 1, 5.

Physicians for Human Rights. (1988, March 30). The casualties of conflict: Medical care and human rights in the West Bank and Gaza Strip. Report of a medical fact-finding mission. Somerville, Mass.: Physicians for Human Rights.

Pines, R. (1989, January 10). Why do Israelis burn out: The role of the Intifada. Paper presented at the International Conference on Psychological Stress and Adjustment, Tel Aviv, Israel.

Punamaki, R. (1987, April). Psychological stress responses of Palestinian mothers and their children in conditions of military occupation and political violence. *Quarterly Newsletter of the Laboratory of Comparative Human Cognition,* 9(2): 76–84.

Pynoos, R., & Eth, S. (1986). Witness to violence: The child interview. *Journal of the American Academy of Child Psychiatry, 25*(3), 306–319.

Rädda Barnen (Swedish Save the Children). (1989, February). Children as targets: A report on military violence against children in the occupied territories in 1988. Stockholm: Rädda Barnen.

Radinsky, L. (1990, April–May). Ten years of revolution: The accomplishments. *Peace and Justice Journal, 9.*

Rayhida, J., Shaya, M., & Armenian, H. (1986). Child health in a city at war. In J. Bryce & H. Armenian (Eds.), *Wartime: The state of children in Lebanon.* Beirut: American University of Beirut.

Reardon, P. (1988, June 22). CHA violent crimes up 9% for year. *Chicago Tribune,* sec. 1, 1.

Reynolds, P. (1989). The impact of apartheid, destabilization, and warfare on children in southern and South Africa. In *Children on the front line.* New York/Geneva: UNICEF.

Robinson, L., & Speck, M. (1990, February 26). Showdown in Nicaragua. *U.S. News and World Report,* 40–41.

Sameroff, A., Seifer, R., Barocas, R., Zax, M., & Greenspan, S. (1987). Intelligence quotient scores of 4-year-old children: Social-environmental risk factors. *Pediatrics, 79,* 343–350.

Secretary's Task Force on Black and Minority Health. (1985) *Report of the Secretary's Task Force on Black and Minority Health. Vol. 1: Executive Summary.* Washington, DC: U. S. Department of Health and Human Services.

Seever, F. (1990). Interview, Chicago.

———. (1990). *Report to the MacArthur Foundation,* unpublished report.

Sharp, G. (1989). The Intifadah and nonviolent struggle. *Journal of Palestine Studies, 19,* 3–13.

Sheehan, N. (1988). *A bright shining lie: John Paul Vann and America in Vietnam.* New York: Random House.

Sheppard, N. (1980, August 6). Chicago project dwellers live under siege. *New York Times,* sec. A, 14.

Sheppard, N. (1990, September 25). Sandinistas snub austerity plan. *Chicago Tribune,* sec. 1, 6.

Silver, E. (1988, September 29). Rabin gives license to wound. *Financial Times,* 6.

Sivard, R. (1989). *World military and social expenditures 1989.* Washington, DC: World Priorities.

Sorensen, V. K. (1945). *Krigens Maend.* Odense, Flensted.

Stanley, A. (1990, June 18). Child warriors. *Time,* 30–52.

Supeta, J. (1990). Interview, Mozambique.

Terry, D. (1990, May 6). Harlem: Death is an old and busy neighborhood. *New York Times,* 18.

Thornton, J. (1988, May 30). After shooting of 9-year-old boy, fear echoes through CHA project. *Chicago Tribune,* sec. 1, 8.

Tully, S. (1989). Children at the center of concern in Nicaragua. Unpublished paper, University of California–Berkeley.

UNICEF. (1986, March 10). *Children in situations of armed conflict.* New York: UNICEF.

UNICEF. (1989). *Children on the front line. The impact of apartheid, destabilization and warfare on children in southern and South Africa.* New York: UNICEF.

UNICEF. (1990). *Interviews with field office staff of education department.* Maputo, Mozambique.

UNICEF, Office of the Special Representative, Phnom Penh. (1990). *Cambodia: The situation of children and women.* New York: UNICEF.

UNICEF, UN, UNDP, UNESCO, and The World Bank. (1990, March 5). World Conference on Education for All. Information Kit. Jomtien, Thailand.

United Nations Development Program (UNDP) and the Government of Mozambique. (1990, December). *Update emergency situation in Mozambique and provisional assessment of 1991 relief needs.* Maputo, Mozambique: UNDP.

United Nations Relief and Works Agency (UNRWA). (1987). *Annual Report of the Director of Health.* Vienna: UNRWA.

Urdang, S. (1989). *And still they dance: Women, war and the struggle for change in Mozambique.* London: Earthscan Publications.

van der Kolk, B. (1987). *Psychological trauma.* Washington, DC: American Psychiatric Press.

Wallerstein, J., & Blakeslee, S. (1989). Second chances: Men, women, and children a decade after divorce. San Francisco: Ticknor & Fields.

Wilson, W. (1987). *The truly disadvantaged.* Chicago: University of Chicago Press.

Wolff, P. (1990). *The orphans of Eritrea.* Boston: Unpublished paper, Judge Baker Children's Center.

World Health Organization (WHO). (1989, May). Needs assessment in respect of emergency medical care in UNRWA clinics and non-government hospitals of the West Bank and Gaza. Geneva: WHO Short Term Consultancy.

Zinsmeister, K. (1990, June). Growing up scared. *Atlantic Monthly,* 49–66.

Index

Abu-Lughod, J., 108
Acker, A., 86, 89, 98
Afghanistan, 8
African Kora, 61, 62
Age of military service, debate over, 11
Alberto, Jorge, 67
American Civil War, youthful ideologues in, 26
Amnesty International, 88, 99
And Quiet Flows the Don (Sholokhov), 55
And Still They Dance (Urdang), 2
Argentina, 23
Armenian, H., 22
Association of Israeli and Palestinian Physicians for Human Rights, 112
Association of Sandinista Children (ANS), 98
Attachments: social support from persons outside the family, 20–22. *See also* Parental attachments

Baker, 126
Bangkok Post, 38
Bell, C., 12, 154
Belske, Carolyn, 69, 73
Berry-Koch, A., 152, 153
Bettelheim, Bruno, 23, 127
Bishop, P., 116, 119
Blakeslee, S., 18
Blau, R., 131, 132, 137, 141
Bliesener, T., 18
Blindness as a coping mechanism, 31–32
Body counts, meaning of, 8
Boothby, N., 73
Bronowski, Jacob, 12
Brothers Karamazov (Dostoyevsky), 83
Burlingham, D., 17, 21
Burns, J., 8, 9

Cambodia: blindness as a coping mechanism in, 31–32; Buddhism and the healing process, 53–54; Commemoration Day, 47, 48; depression in survivors, 43–44; description of Khmer Rouge and Pol Pot in, 36–37, 39–41; description of life in Phnom Penh, 51–53; description of refugee camps in, 44–46; example of a child's response to violence, 4; Feeding Center example, 49–50; future of, 58–59; history of, 38; how children made sense of the senseless, 48–51; impaired memory in survivors, 48; impressment of children, 16, 41; indoctrination methods used for coping, 41; infant mortality rate in, 40, 42; orphans in, 57; parallel to other cultures and reasons for the killings in, 54–56; rebuilding of, 56–58; return of the Khmer Rouge in, 37–38; role of Thailand in, 44–45; role of the U.S. in, 38–39, 42–43; role of the Vietnamese in, 42; sense of mission in survivors, 46–48; symptoms of post traumatic stress disorder, 22; tower of skulls in, 32–34; Tuol Sleng prison, 40
Caseso, J., 131, 132
Catch 22 (Heller), 7
Chamorro, Violeta, 91
Cheung, Sindy, xviii
Chicago: children as perpetrators of crime in, 141–142; children as victims of crime in, 136–138; crime in the developments, 131–133, 135–136; education in, 133–134; examples of responses to violence, 138–140, 147; future of individuals in, 145–149; health care in, 134; importance of parental attachments, 17–18; life in the developments, 134–136; problems confronted by parents, 142–143; problems confronted by professionals, 143–145; rate at which children are exposed to violent crime, 136; role of play in, 12–13; Taylor Homes, 131, 133; as a war zone, 12

Chicago Community Mental Health Council, 136
Chicago Housing Authority, 133, 135, 146
Chicago Sun Times, 132
Chicago Tribune, 115
Child: abuse in Palestine, 121–122; Convention on the Rights of the, 10, 11, 123, 154–157; how to protect a, 162–163, 165; neglect in Palestine, 122–124; rights of a, 159–161; what it means to be a, 9–13
Chile, 23
Chilton, R., 131
Chorn, Arn, 31, 32
CIA, 98, 99
Cockburn, A., 90, 99
Cohen, C. P., 11, 154
Coles, Robert, 27, 49
Community, role of the, 20–22
Contras, attacks from the, 88–89, 92–95
Convention on the Rights of the Child, 10, 11, 123, 154–157
Coping: blindness as a coping mechanism, 31–32; importance of listening to children, 28–30; indoctrination methods used in Cambodia for, 41; statistics on, 29–30; with stress, 18–19
Coping, factors that affect: cognitive competence, 19; experiences of self-efficacy, 19; open, supportive educational climate, 19–20; social support from persons outside the family, 20–22; stable emotional relationships, 19

DataBase Project on Palestinian Human Rights, 114, 115, 116, 117, 120, 122
Davidson, H., 11, 154
DeAngelis, T., 31, 32
Dehumanization, 22–23
Demonization, 22–23
Depression in survivors in Cambodia, 43–44
Dodd, Christopher, 151
Don Flows Quietly to the Sea, The, (Sholokhov), 55
Dostoyevsky, Fyodor, 83
Dubrow, N., 136, 142
Dyson, J., 139

Edelman, M., 133
Educational climate: in Chicago, 133–134; importance of, 19–20; in Mozambique,

65–67; in Nicaragua, 86, 90; in Palestine and Occupied Territories, 110, 113–115
Erikson, Erik, 10
Erikson Institute, 28, 144, 165
Eritrea, 153–154
Eth, S., 136

Famine in Mozambique, 64–65, 69
FBI, 130
Federal Laboratories, 121
Financial Times, 120
Finkelhor, David, 10–11
Fish-Murray, C., 30
Frente Sandinista de Liberacion Nacional (FSLN), 86. *See also* Sandinista National Liberation Front
Freud, Anna, 17, 18, 21
Front for the Liberation of Mozambique (FRELIMO), creation of, 61
Fuerza Democratica Nicaraguense (FDN), 88

Gang(s): crime committed by, 130–131; growth of, 130, 131; weaponry, 132; wilding, 141
Gannon, J., 86, 88
Garbarino, J., 23, 28, 136, 142
Gardner, G., 134
Germany, youthful ideologues in Nazi, 26
Gramezy, Norman, 76
Gross, J., 131, 143
Gulf Crisis, 161–162

Handicap International, 35
Harlem, 135
Health care: in Chicago, 134; in Nicaragua, 86–87; in Palestine and Occupied Territories, 110, 112–113, 124
Heller, Joseph, 7
Horton, Myles, 25

Ideology: children and, 26–28; role of, 22–25
Illinois Criminal Justice Information Authority, 134
Illinois Department of Children and Family Services (IDCFS), 137
Impressment of children: in Cambodia, 16, 41; in Mozambique, 16, 63; in Nicaragua, 97
In'ash al-Usra, 115

Infant mortality rate: in Cambodia, 40, 42; in Mozambique, 64; in Nicaragua, 86; in Palestine and Occupied Territories, 110

Infantario Provincial Orphanage, 73

Inhambane Hospital, description of, 68–73

International Catholic Child Bureau (Geneva), 80

Intifada: game played by children, 12; impact of growing up in the, 126–129; meaning of word, 104. *See also* Palestine and Occupied Territories

Iran, youthful ideologues in, 26

Israel: casualties suffered by, 118; example of moral sensibility, 27; examples of violence against Palestine, 108–109; role of fundamentalist groups in, 24; rule over Palestine, 107–108; Six Day War, 108; use of rubber/plastic bullets against Palestinian children, 119–120; use of tear gas against Palestinian children, 120–121; violence against Palestinian children, 116–119; youthful ideologues in, 26

Jackson, R., 71

Jalazon refugee camp, 12

Janis, I., 127

Jerusalem Post, 113, 114, 122

Jones, Marion, 72, 73

Karnow, S., 56

Kelly, H., 71

Khmer Rouge: description of, 36–37, 39–41; return of, 37–38. *See also* Cambodia

Kidnapping by strangers, statistics on, 3

Kiernan, B., 39

Kifner, J., 119

Killing Fields, The, 41–42

Kinzer, S., 89

Kinzie, J. D., 22

Kotulak, R., 136

Lane, C., 100

Laos, impact of U.S. weapons on, 35

Lebanon, symptoms of post traumatic stress disorder in, 22

Lewis, C. S., 55

Lösel, F., 18

McCallin, M., 67, 80

Machel, Samora, 64

McMullen, M., 90

Malnutrition: impact of, 150–151; in Mozambique, 64–65, 69, 71–72, 150–151; in Nicaragua, 90. *See also* Health care

Manifest Destiny, 84, 98

Marin, C., 138, 142

Massacre at Mueda, 61

Memory, impaired: in Cambodian survivors, 48; in Mozambique survivors, 72–73

Metraux, J., 87, 90

Mondlane, Eduardo, 61

Monroe Doctrine, 84, 98

Moral sensibility, development of, 27–28

Morganthau, T., 132

Mozambique: assault on teachers in, 65–66, 67; creation and influence of Renamo, 62–63, 66; creation of FRELIMO, 61; description of atrocities committed by Renamo, 70–71, 72, 74, 78–79; description of Inhambane Hospital, 68–73; description of life in Maputo, 65; education in, 65–67; example of a child's response to violence, 4–5; family life in Maxixe/Rumbana, Inhambane, 77–79; famine in, 64–65, 69; future of, 81–82; games still played in, 81; history of, 60–61; impaired memory in survivors, 72–73; impressment of children, 16, 63; infant mortality rate in, 64; Infantario Provincial, 73; malnutrition in, 64–65, 69, 71–72, 150–151; Massacre at Mueda, 61; moral/political meanings for killings, 63–64; orphans in, 73–77; psychological need, 79–81; statistics on the death of children in, 63–64; street children in Maputo, 67–68; Support Network, 160; torture of children in, 67; Xai Xai Orphanage, 75–77

Mozambique National Resistance (MNR), 62

Mullen, W., 45, 153

Nam, Kik, 63

National Association of Housing Redevelopment Officials, 132, 136

National Commission on Stressed Public Housing, 133

National Opposition Union (UNO), 91

Nazi concentration camps, role of ideology in, 23–24

Nelson, H., 89, 90

New York City Departments of Planning and Health, 135
New York Times, 116
Nicaragua: attacks from the Contras, 88–89, 92–95; education in, 86, 90; examples of responses to violence, 4, 97–98; future of, 99–100; girl's story of events, 92–95; Guardia, 88; health care in, 86–87; history of, 84–86; housing shortage in, 91; impact of war on children, 84, 88–91; impressment of children in, 97; infant mortality rate in, 86; life in Matagalpa, 95–97; malnutrition in, 90; psychological trauma in, 90; relocation of orphans, 87–88; role of the U.S. in, 84–85, 90, 91–92, 98–100; under the Sandinistas, 86–87, 91–92
Nixon, A., 112, 113, 116, 118, 119, 120, 121, 123, 125
Nkomati Accord, 62
Nol, Lon, 38
Nyambir, Jacob, 66

Occupied Territories. *See* Palestine and Occupied Territories
Ogintz, E., 142, 145
Organization of the Revolutionary Disabled (ORD), 98
Ortega, Daniel, 91

Padgett, T., 100
Palestine and Occupied Territories: arrest of children, 116–117; British rule of, 106–107; child abuse in, 121–122; child neglect in, 122–124; demolition or sealing of houses in, 112; education in, 110, 113–115; effect of curfews on children, 113, 125; emigration of Palestinians, 125–126; example of moral sensibility, 27–28; examples of Israeli violence against, 108–109; examples of responses to violence, 127–129; health care in, 110, 112–113, 124; history of, 104–108; impact of growing up in the *Intifada*, 126–129; infant mortality rate in, 110; Israeli rule of, 107–108; life in the refugee camps, 109–110; location of, 101–103; massacre in Deir Yassin, 107; role of fundamentalist groups in, 24–25; role of play in, 12; Temple Mount-Haram al-Sharif, 105, 118, 158; Uprising, 104, 108; use of rubber/plastic bullets against

children, 119–120; use of tear gas against children, 120–121; violence conducted against children, 115–119; voluntary fighting by children in, 16, 123, 124; youthful ideologues in, 26–27
Palestine Liberation Organization (PLO), 102
Parental attachments: ability to cope and, 19; impact of war on, 17–18; importance of, 10, 19
Patton, George, 15
Phnom Penh, description of life in, 51–53
Physicians for Human Rights, 122
Pines, R., 24
Play, importance of, 11–12
Pol Pot, 36, 37, 38, 55
Post traumatic stress disorder (PTSD), 21–22
Psychic toll in adulthood, 18
Psychological aid, need for, 153–154
Punamaki, Raija-Leena, 26–27, 127
Pynoos, R., 136

Rabin, Yitzak, 120, 122
Rädda Barnen, 116, 120
Radinsky, L., 86, 88
Rayhida, J., 22
Reagan administration, 92
Reardon, P., 135
Refugees, statistics on, 152–153
Renamo: attacks on teachers, 66, 67; creation and influence of, 62–63; description of atrocities committed by, 70–71, 72, 74, 78–79
Reynolds, P., 67
Robinson, L., 90

Sameroff, A., 134
Sandinista National Liberation Front: creation of, 86; reforms under, 86–87
Sandino, Cesar Augusto, 85
Saucasa, Juan Bautista, 85
Save the Children, 43, 73, 112, 116, 118, 119
Secretary's Task Force on Black and Minority Health Executive Summary, 131
Seever, F., 131, 132, 141
Sharp, G., 105
Shaw, George Bernard, 43
Shaya, M., 22
Sheehan, N., 43
Sheppard, N., 133

Shin Beth agents, 115
Sholokhov, Mikhail, 55
Sihanouk, Prince Norodom, 38
Sivard, R., 130
Six Day War, 108
Social dislocation, 150
Society for the Preservation of the Family, 115
Somoza, Anastasio, 85, 88
Sorensen, V. K., xii
Stanley, A., 145
Stott, F., 28
Supeta, J., 60

Taylor Homes, Robert. *See* Chicago
Teenagers, impact of war on, 17
Terry, D., 135
Thailand, Cambodia and role of, 44–45
That Hideous Strength (Lewis), 55
Thornton, J., 137
Torture of children: in Chile, 23; in Mozambique, 67
TransTechnology Corp., 121
Tully, S., 87
Tuol Sleng prison, 40

Ullmann, Liv, 42, 151
UNICEF, 163; Cambodia and, 36, 39, 40, 42, 57; Mozambique and, 62, 64, 66, 67; statistics on casualties of war, 1, 14
United Nations: Convention on the Rights of the Child, 10, 11, 123, 154–157; statistics on refugees, 152–153; Summit on Children, 156
United Nations Relief and Works Agency (UNWRA), 110, 122
United States: Cambodia and role of the, 38–39, 42–43; growth of gangs in the, 130; homeless in the, 153; homicide rate in the, 131; impact of U.S. weapons on Laos, 35; Nicaragua and role of the, 84–85, 90, 91–92, 98–100; poverty line in the, 133; U.S. Senate Subcommittee on Children, 151
Urdang, Stephanie, 2

van der Kolk, B., 18
Vietnam: Cambodia and, 42; impact of U.S. weapons on, 34–35; youthful ideologues in, 26
Voluntary fighting by children, 16

Walker, William, 85
Wallerstein, J., 18
War: definitions of, 5–8, 130; economic impact of, 9; gradations of bestiality, 158–159; impact of, on children, 17–18; impact of, on teenagers, 17; just/good war versus unjust/bad war, 157
Wiesel, Elie, x
Wilding, 141
Wilson, W., 133
Wolff, P., 153
World Health Organization, 124
World War I, 43
World War II: importance of parental attachments, 17, 21; psychic toll in adulthood, 18

Xai Xai Orphanage, 75–77

Youth for Peace, 31

Zinsmeister, K., 130, 132, 136, 141

About the
Authors

James Garbarino is codirector of the Family Life Development Center and professor of Human Development at Cornell University. He served as president of the Erikson Institute for Advanced Study in Child Development from 1985 to 1994. He has undertaken special missions for UNICEF to assess the impact of the Gulf War on children in Kuwait and Iraq and has served as a consultant for programs serving Bosnian and Croatian children. Garbarino is the author or editor of seventeen books including *Understanding Abusive Families* (1997, second edition), *Raising Children in a Socially Toxic Environment* (1995), *Let's Talk About Living in a World with Violence* (1993), and *Children in Danger: Coping with the Consequences of Community Violence* (1992). Garbarino has also been a consultant on numerous television, magazine, and newspaper reports on children and families. An internationally recognized expert on child-abuse prevention and social policy issues, Garbarino has been the recipient of many awards in recognition of his efforts on behalf of children. In 1995 he was awarded an honorary Doctor of Humane Letters by St. Lawrence University.

Kathleen Kostelny is senior research associate and director of the Project on Children and Violence at the Erikson Institute in Chicago. She has written numerous articles on children and violence and serves as a consultant to national and international organizations concerned with the impact of political and community violence on children. She currently chairs the task force on Children in War and Community Violence of the Division of Peace Psychology of the American Psychological Association. In 1992 she was honored with James Garbarino by the Society for the Psychological Study of Social Issues for her work "Child Maltreatment as a Community

Problem," and in 1995 she was named a National Fellow by the W.K. Kellogg Foundation.

Nancy Dubrow is founder and director of the International Child Welfare Group of the Taylor Institute in Chicago. She is a pioneer in addressing the psychosocial effects of violence on children and has written numerous publications on the topic. She is the United Nations representative to UNICEF for the World Federation for Mental Health and an expert in human development, diplomacy, and advocacy on behalf of children worldwide.